"What a g... Brian Barcelona has g...
the profound stories of what God is doing on campus...
The Jesus Club will ignite within you a greater passion
for Jesus and an unstoppable faith to see God move
in the lives of students. Hearing the stories of what
God has done and is doing in our day is critical if we
are to move from just talking about revival to actually
seeing a generation changed by the love and power of
God."

Banning Liebscher, founder and pastor,
Jesus Culture

"Brian Barcelona is seeing America's schools set ablaze
with the Fire of God. What he teaches he has lived and
continues to model. This book will provoke, challenge
and inspire you. It will give you fresh faith to see the
next generation won to Christ."

Daniel Kolenda, president and CEO,
Christ for all Nations

"What you are about to read can only be understood
as storyline straight from the pen of the Author of our
faith. For years at TheCall gatherings we have cried
out for a young generation to encounter Jesus. I believe
this is one dramatic answer to the cries of thousands.
Brian Barcelona and a company of young students have
believed for the impossible and dared to step into it.
Read and watch hope explode in your soul. God's not
done with America!"

Lou Engle, co-founder, TheCall

"Though young in years, Brian Barcelona reminds me of a modern-day David. Preaching in the high schools of America? That's a crazy idea! Yet by taking simple steps of obedience, Brian walks through the spiritual strongholds and sees doors open where you would least expect them. Truly, with God, all things are possible. Let this book challenge you about what can happen when you put your hope and trust in Jesus and step out in faith just as Brian did."

Loren Cunningham, founder, Youth With A Mission

"God places favor on people's lives for the task at hand. This favor has been placed on Brian Barcelona and the One Voice Student Missions team. I have been involved with and have seen Brian's passion for students to know about Jesus! It is absolutely amazing what is happening in the high schools right now! If you ever have felt hopeless about our school system in America, this is a must-read!"

Todd White, president, Lifestyle Christianity, lifestylechristianity.com

"My senior year of high school I had no idea about who God was until I stepped into Laguna Creek High's auditorium. That day I was introduced to Brian, and from there forward, his guidance helped mold me into the man I am today. Since knowing Brain I've built a strong relationship with God. I've slipped and fallen a thousand times and I will probably fall a thousand more, but now I know through my faith that you can always get back up. This book is powerful, and it can change your life in the way Brian changed mine."

Don Jackson, NFL running back,
Green Bay Packers

"*The Jesus Club* chronicles the miracle journey of a movement that is significantly impacting the youth of California. Brian Barcelona writes with the passion of a man who has been encountered by Jesus and His heart for the lost. In this book are the seeds of campus revivals all over America."

Jude Fouquier, pastor, The City Church Ventura

"I met Brian Barcelona during the summer of 2010. Brian was a very energetic, personable and sincere person, and I was immediately taken by his passion for helping high school kids. Over the following two years, Brian's presence on campus had a positive impact on our students and staff. Brian's deep faith and trust in God, combined with his taking time to listen to kids and meet them where they are in life, is why his clubs make a difference."

Doug Craig, high school principal

"Brian has brilliantly presented how the Lord can take broken individuals and weave lives, circumstances and obedience to the glory of His name. I watched the Gospel come to life and realized Brian's messages were impacting countless lives. In this season, a new boldness and faith grew in me that I had never known before.

May the message in this book become the launching mechanism for you that it was for me."

Eric Johnson, teacher, Laguna Creek High School

"Something supernatural was birthed the day Brian Barcelona encountered God at a conference, and ever since he has had a passion for students. If you desire to be on campuses reaching students with Jesus' love, *The Jesus Club* will help propel you to take that next step. Brian provides simple and effective tools to getting on the campuses and staying encouraged as you continue. As you read, be inspired and let the Holy Spirit lead you as you seek to reach the students in your city."

Jeremy Johnson, lead pastor, Fearless LA Church

THE JESUS CLUB

INCREDIBLE TRUE STORIES OF HOW GOD IS MOVING IN OUR HIGH SCHOOLS

BRIAN BARCELONA

Chosen

a division of Baker Publishing Group
Minneapolis, Minnesota

© 2017 by Brian Barcelona

Published by Chosen Books
11400 Hampshire Avenue South
Bloomington, Minnesota 55438
www.chosenbooks.com

Chosen Books is a division of
Baker Publishing Group, Grand Rapids, Michigan

Printed in the United States of America

Library of Congress Cataloging-in-Publication Data
Names: Barcelona, Brian, author.
Title: The Jesus club : incredible true stories of how God is moving in
    our high schools / Brian Barcelona.
Description: Minneapolis, Minnesota : Chosen, 2017.
Identifiers: LCCN 2016040244 | ISBN 9780800798192 (trade paper :
    alk. paper)
Subjects: LCSH: High school students—Religious life. | Church work
    with teenagers.
Classification: LCC BV4531.3 .B358 2017 | DDC 267/.61—dc23
LC record available at https://lccn.loc.gov/2016040244

Scripture quotations are from the New American Standard Bible®, copyright © 1960, 1962, 1963, 1968, 1971, 1972, 1973, 1975, 1977, 1995 by The Lockman Foundation. Used by permission. (www.Lockman.org)

The names of certain individuals have been changed in order to protect their privacy.

Photographs by Manuel Gaitan. Used by permission.

Cover design by Gearbox

17 18 19 20 21 22 23   7 6 5 4 3 2 1

This book is dedicated first to the Lord, for all He has taught me and all He has allowed me to be part of.

Second I want to dedicate this book to my amazing wife, Marcela, for her constant encouragement and the love she has shown me, always pointing me to hear God in everything I do, and to my beautiful daughter, Zoe, who I know will change her nation one day.

CONTENTS

9

CONTENTS

FOREWORD

THE STORY OF HOW GOD HAS USED Brian Barcelona in high school campuses through One Voice Student Missions is one that has changed the lives of thousands of students across the country. I personally have seen and believe that now more than ever there is a window of opportunity that we must seize to reach the youth of this nation right where they are every day. The awakening of local churches to reach youth is happening like never before, and everyone is asking, "How do we reach the next generation?"

One Voice Student Missions is wisely and strategically using the local church as a focal point to sponsor the mission field where the Good News still can be shared. While that window remains open, now is the time of salvation and discipleship! This book is one I would recommend you read—to get inspired but also to realize what is possible and that you can live out these stories in your city campuses as well. You will be moved and challenged, not to just sit back in the church seats as "consumers," but to be moved, to *go* and *love* students unconditionally. If you're a student, pastor or leader, I encourage everyone to see this model and book of testimonies as a way that we as the body can be unified in our vision to see Jesus lifted high for all to see!

Nick Vujicic, president, Life Without Limbs

ACKNOWLEDGMENTS

I WOULD LIKE TO THANK DAD AND MOM and Grandma Arlene for their support and love. Where would I be without the prayers of my grandma and the love of my parents?

Papa Lou Engle and Mama Therese, thank you for always being godly examples and teaching me to believe God and never take anything less than revival in my generation.

My pastors, Netz and Lourdes, thank you for the time you have invested in me, always teaching me to do nothing but from prayer. You have been the greatest example of leadership to me.

Grandma Willi, the woman who dared to believe America would be saved, thank you. The many talks and love and support changed my life forever.

And last but not least, my One Voice family. Thank you for the time and countless hours you have spent with me going to these high schools and living out these stories. Thank you for your sold-out lives to Jesus and your incredible friendship. This would never have been possible without you guys.

INTRODUCTION

The philosophy of the classroom in one generation will be the philosophy of government in the next.

ANONYMOUS

YOUNG PEOPLE HAVE MANY VIEWS OF Jesus. Some have been taught He does not exist; others say He is a historical figure only. Others validate His existence but deny His power as alive and active today.

I want to share with you the story of the Jesus students are meeting in their high schools: the Jesus who touches their lives; the Jesus who heals their families both spiritually and physically; the Jesus who saves them from hell right in their gyms and auditoriums and theaters during lunchtime, every week; the Jesus who is not afraid of the separation of church and state; the Jesus who goes beyond four walls and a pulpit to the school grounds and classrooms.

In the next fifteen to twenty years, I believe we will see and hear amazing new voices that God will be using in nations throughout the world. When asked where their salvation took place, their response will sound like this: "I got saved in a gym on a campus during lunch." When asked the name of the speaker, they will reply, "I don't know. All I know is, I met Jesus."

I have heard stories of people who met Jesus in church, and others who met Him at a Christian conference, and still others who met Him on the streets. This story is about students who met Jesus in a Bible club.

The Jesus Club.

1

SUMMER
OF CHANGE

T WAS A HOT SUMMER DAY IN JULY 2009. Little did I know that the youth gathering I was heading to would change my life forever. The bus ride felt normal. Our church youth group was laughing and sharing crazy stories as we drove the bumpy road to Santa Cruz, California, to a huge weekend event with some of the best Christian bands and speakers from across the country. This gathering was called Spirit West Coast. And in no way was I prepared for what God was about to invite me into.

For the previous year and a half I had been enjoying the simple fact that I had met Jesus and was free from my life of brokenness. I loved reading my Bible every day as I learned more about who Jesus was. Though I was only sixteen when I was saved, I fell instantly in love with God and wanted to do all He had for me to do. I made it my goal never to miss anything my church was part of, whether a prayer meeting, a youth night or a conference. I felt a sense of urgency within me not to miss His voice.

Within Spirit West Coast were smaller events, such as Ammunition Conference, which was led by a good friend of mine, Pastor Jeremy Johnson. The name did it justice. Every session seemed to spark something powerful in my life. I was hungry to learn from the experiences of the men and women who spoke from the platform in that huge white tent, wondering in my heart if I, too, would ever have stories like theirs.

With more than a thousand high school and college students listening to speakers and enjoying the different bands, the question ran through my mind quite often of whether or not God even noticed me. But the first night I found myself weeping during the altar call, watching as students made their way to the front for prayer. God was encountering me, and I was feeling passionate about the salvation of my friends and family back home.

Up to this point in my life, I had never felt a calling to go into high schools and talk about Jesus; I only wanted to see my friends saved. I was trying to find ways to serve Jesus faithfully—reading my Bible every second I could and loving the people He put into my life. Oh—and leading worship for our youth group was my favorite. All the worship songs that seemed old to some of the other kids were new to me, seeing as I had not been saved long. My faith felt so fresh and alive I could not imagine the flame ever being snuffed out.

The next day, with the afternoon session finishing up, I felt the need to be alone with God and try to talk with Him about my life. As the band began playing the last song, I got up quietly from my seat in the front and made my way toward the few empty chairs at the back of the tent. I was hoping no one would notice me and think I was not interested in joining the worship, but the urgency in my heart kept my feet moving.

Once I sat in the back and started to talk to God, my heart began to beat faster than normal. Within seconds I noticed that everything around me—the worship team and their instruments, the natural shuffling and movement of so many people clapping and singing—began to quiet down as if someone was turning down the sound of life. As I simply waited to see what would happen next, I heard God speaking clearly to me within my heart. His voice was gentle yet filled with power.

As I listened closely the Lord said, *Brian, I want to release a movement that will save the high schools of America. And I want to use your life to do it. This movement will take your city. It will take California. So goes California, so goes the nation.*

I felt almost shocked. I had no words, but tears flooded my eyes and spilled down my cheeks. The realization that I was a new Christian came quickly to try to rob me of the words God was speaking to me. Plus, I was just eighteen now! How could God entrust me with such a thing?

I was weeping uncontrollably, my hands covering my eyes and my head bowed in awe of God. I felt my heart being filled with the faith that I would need if I were to walk the long road the Lord had just laid out in front of me.

God continued to speak: *The movement I am about to release is going to restore prayer in the public schools again.*

At once everything went back to normal. I could hear the joyful singing and shouting of a thousand young people worshiping God.

I sat in the back of the huge white tent and continued to cry, overwhelmed at what I had just heard. I knew it was God. It was like a stern order from a general to a soldier, yet His words also felt like a father asking his son for a favor. Even though the moment was intense, I knew one thing to be true: I had a choice whether or not to obey. God had interrupted my life, and I could let it remain an interruption or let it become an invitation.

But even if I chose to obey, would God really use me in His plan to bring revival to America's high schools? How would I even approach such a thing? Campuses were not a passion of mine. Nothing in the natural world led me to think God was going to save high schools. There was also nothing in the natural that led me to think God could possibly use me to help do it.

I stood up still dazed by what had taken place and yet surprised that no one else seemed to have heard what I had heard. I had only a vague blueprint from God, since He had left out the many details of my journey. I knew that He wanted to save high schools and that He wanted me to have a role in it.

The only high school campus I had any connection with was the one I had just graduated from a year earlier—Elk Grove High. It made sense to think about starting there.

So as soon as the worship ended, feeling excited yet a little afraid, I found one of my friends, an older guy whom I trusted, and began to tell him what had just happened. With passion and excitement, I poured out word after word of what God had said.

He listened and seemed careful not to quench my passion. Here I was, after all, this teenager telling him that God was going to save every high school in America. I realized at that moment that this assignment from the Lord might not affect others the same way it had affected me.

When I finished pouring out my heart, he looked at me with a smile and said simply, "If God told you, do it."

I knew he was right. Despite feeling a little alone and not understood, I said yes to God that day in that tent and in my heart, not knowing that my yes would lead to thousands of students being saved. I didn't go kneel at an altar or answer a preacher's call to ministry. But that day I accepted an assignment from heaven. It might have been given to many others who might not have said yes, but I did. And though it was a weak yes, it would show much fruit in the years to come.

As the weekend gathering continued, my friends and I hung out hearing all kinds of Christian bands. When the last song was finished, we headed back to our campsite for the saddest part of the trip: packing our things and going home. As I gathered my clothes and belongings, I kept thinking of what would come next. It was still summer but school was soon to start.

Hours later we arrived back in Elk Grove. I knew something was different. I had never felt love for my city the way I did that evening when we drove in. I had felt love for people before, but never for a geographical location. Yes, this may sound weird, but it was as if the dirt lot and the park and the high schools now had a place in my heart because this was where God had put me.

And for the first time my heart had compassion and love for the young people in the high schools who didn't know Jesus. My life was ruined for the dreams I had previously, like pursuing music and going to college. Even the dream of driving a nice car didn't seem that important.

My mom greeted me when I got home, so I started telling her everything that God had told me. She stood there listening to all I had to say only to reply with her famous smile accompanied by her famous Mom-saying: "That's good, *hijo*," which is Spanish for *son*.

After dinner I went to my room and began to pray for the Lord's words to come true. My heart was filled with joy yet uncertainty—not uncertainty that God had spoken but wondering how all this would come to pass. How was God going to use my life to reach every high school in the nation?

"Send me to the high schools!" became my prayer. It was almost like a weight on my heart when I thought about the kids who did not know Jesus.

The rest of that summer I contemplated how and when I would start. Since I had no clue what to do or model to follow, I kept praying for Him to guide me. At one point, I actually sensed some direction from God. I was reading in the gospels about how Jesus made disciples and how it took *an action*, not just *a wanting*, on their part. I knew I had to take the first step. Any step, even in the wrong direction, was better than no step, because I knew if God was this faithful to speak then He would take me the way I needed to go.

I was willing to put aside the wants and desires of my "self" in order to obey the Lord. I was willing to do whatever He asked because I knew He would never ask me to start something He was not going to complete. Since I had not been saved long, I did not have much history with God—both in the sense of serving Him and in the sense of seeing Him coming through in my life. But I did have instant trust that He would never let me down. God would not wait sixteen years to pull my life out of depression and thoughts of suicide and then give me a directive that was way beyond my abilities—just to let me fail.

And as one of the speakers had said at the conference, if you can accomplish the dreams in your heart by yourself, then they are probably not from God. I knew for certain that in no way could I pull this one off.

In the days leading up to the start of school, I stayed faithful and committed to my youth group, leading worship, while still keeping this dream of God close to my heart. That time really prepped and taught me about following the word of the Lord and also about His timing. Faith without works is dead, I knew, but the timing of God would be what allowed the works to show my faith as alive.

I spent much time in prayer and fasting. Since I could not hear Him much about what to do next, I learned that serving Jesus and walking out what He speaks went beyond my feelings and emotions. It got down to the core of my obedience.

Regardless of how I thought those prayer times were going, God honored them; in fact, I had the sense that the fruit I was to see in the following years might be traced to those times of praying and fasting. I also realized something else: that I needed Jesus just as much as the kids in high schools did. Nothing, therefore, depended on my skill. Everything depended on His willingness to move and my willingness to obey. Fifteen hundred-plus kids at Elk Grove High were about to enter their campus and my mission field. God was sending me on a rescue mission. This venture would not take a week or a month; it would be the start of a lifetime journey.

I grew nervous as the start date of school drew closer. How would I even get back on campus since I had already graduated? And what would I say? I might sound crazy even to the students, let alone the administration. And to top everything off, my parents did not serve the Lord and could not fathom why I would plan to go back to high school during the week instead of getting a job or going to college.

I have to admit that the American dream—which I pictured as a nice house with a picket fence and a savings account in the bank—did not tempt me. I was not after that. I was after making Jesus famous at Elk Grove High.

But even though the "good life" did not tempt me, it was hard realizing that no one understood me. That season was my Garden of Gethsemane place, meaning I was standing between a silent God and sleeping people who didn't seem to hear me. It was that moment when my will and God's could possibly collide.

I was not one who needed a million confirmations to do what God had asked me to do, but I am not going to lie: When I felt particularly alone, I would ask Him if I really was to go. And His answer was the same every time: Silence.

Gradually I began to understand that I was asking Him if I should do what He had already told me to do. I knew deep down in my soul I was to go. So I finally decided that I would no longer entertain thoughts of not going—which I admit I had been doing.

His silence screamed *Go*.

To help me through those days, I would close my eyes and hear His words again. Over and over I would replay them in my mind as though it were my first time hearing them. By the time school was starting I had readied myself to do all that God was asking of me.

To be honest, He was not asking all that much. All He was asking of me was to go. I didn't have to be good at anything; I only had to be available. All the pressure of performing seemed to go away. Besides, there wasn't anyone in the city of Elk Grove at that time going into the schools and preaching, so it made my job a whole lot easier.

I cannot tell you the exact date that I walked into Elk Grove High, but I do remember what happened. After parking my 1990 Acura with no AC in the staff parking lot, I went through the blue gates of the school, passing the large metal elk out front—the same elk I had passed many times as a student.

Classes were in session, but it was nearing lunchtime. It felt odd to be in school, still in jeans and a T-shirt, and not be a student. At the same time, memories flooded my mind—memories both good and bad.

See, when I had first come onto the campus as a sophomore, I was a professing atheist; a lot of my experiences there reflected my life before I knew Christ. Now I was approaching the same security guards whom I used to cuss out and give problems to. Hoping they would remember the change in me my senior year, and how I was not so rude anymore, I spoke politely, asking to go to the main office. I was grateful that they nodded and replied, "Go ahead," and let me in.

I had about ten minutes before that familiar school bell would ring signaling lunch. I walked as fast as I could to the front office not really having a plan; I simply talked to the ladies at the front office to see what would happen.

"Excuse me," I said.

One of the women looked up. "Yes? How may we help you?"

"I'm here to meet with the Bible club." I knew there was a club because in my senior year I had seen kids with their Bibles hanging out together during lunch.

The woman nodded. "Mr. Brad Schottle is the one you need to speak to," she replied. "His classroom is in the back of the school, where the portables are. Room

P6. Sign in and take this visitor's pass, and you can head back there."

I knew where those portable classrooms were since my English and math classes had been held there. But I never would have dreamed in a million years that I would be walking toward those same portables with a mission from God.

The bell rang as I pushed open the door and walked back into the bright sunlight. Watching the students pouring out of the portables, whether walking alone lost in thought or chatting with friends and heading for the quad, made me realize for the first time that there was a harvest in high school campuses ready to be gathered. That harvest was *ripe*. It was as if my eyes were opened and I could see the great potential of what the Lord could do.

I walked up the hollow wooden ramp to room P6 and knocked on the door. As I opened it slowly, a medium-sized man with grayish hair looked up from the papers in his hand and greeted me with a smile as I entered the room.

"Can I help you?"

"Hello," I replied. "My name is Brian Barcelona. I want to know if I can speak to Mr. Schottle."

The man nodded. "I am he. How may I help you?"

Now was the moment I had been preparing for ever since God spoke His words into my heart during the youth rally. I began to share with Mr. Schottle how I was a former student of Elk Grove High, and how God had spoken to me. I told him that I wanted to give students the Gospel, since no one had ever given it to me in my high school days.

I poured my heart out regarding the experience I had had with God at Spirit West Coast. I told him about the word God had given me about the high schools of America. I spoke passionately, hoping Mr. Schottle would see my heart for the campus. I was certain that my obedience in the face of such an impossible task would put the demand on God to fulfill His plan.

When I had explained as best I could, I fell silent and waited. Mr. Schottle wore the puzzled look of someone who has no idea how to respond. And quite frankly, I understood. What would you say if a teenager barged into your math room during lunch one day and started talking about what Jesus had told him?

The silence lasted a bit longer, until he nodded slowly.

"Okay," he said finally. "What if you come once a week and speak to the Bible club?"

I knew in my heart that I needed to be on that campus more than once a week to influence it. How I knew I couldn't say, but something inside me said once was not enough.

So I replied in a shaky voice, "What if I come twice a week?"

Again he stood silently, looking at me. It was his decision administratively—and he would be the one held accountable. Finally he said, "You may come every week, twice a week."

A smile that must have looked both relieved and happily goofy spread over my face.

I got the details about which days to come—Tuesday and Wednesday—thanked him, and threw my arms around his shoulders in a hug. I was turning to leave when he spoke again.

"Wait. You have one more thing to do. You've got to check this with the Bible club president. Her name is Kendall. She'll be coming in here in a few minutes."

"Of course!" I replied—as though I knew I had to meet with her.

Not three minutes passed before the classroom door creaked open and a girl carrying a tuba walked in.

"Hello! My name is Brian," I said, hoping this was Kendall.

"Hi. My name is Kendall."

"Perfect!" I said.

She lowered her tuba to the floor and looked from me to Mr. Schottle with some confusion. So I wasted no time. I started to tell her everything I had just told Mr. Schottle.

When my flow of words finally stopped, she asked me a couple of questions and then, after a pause, said with sincerity, "You can speak here."

I was overwhelmed with joy.

I did hear God! I thought.

"I'll see you next week," I said. "Gather as many as you can!"

And then I quickly made my exit. I was trying not to seem too excited, although on the inside I was jumping like crazy.

God had actually opened a door for me to walk through. He had given me a way to reach students—something that only twenty minutes earlier had seemed almost impossible. I had stepped out and He had stepped in.

The next seven days went by fast as I began preparing something to say to the club. But as I woke that Tuesday morning, I knew this was the day that would be written in the history books of my heart.

2

GOD SHOWS UP

AND SO THE JOURNEY BEGAN. I WAS now co-laboring with Kendall and Mr. Schottle. Two people who had been strangers were now becoming friends in what God was going to do. We had one mission: to see the Bible club—the Jesus Club—used as a tool for salvation. All we needed now was for students to come.

Once again I was at the front office signing in and getting my visitor's badge, one of thousands of badges I would wear in the future. I rushed back to room P6 in the portable classroom, greeted Mr. Schottle and waited.

The lunch bell rang. The door opened. In walked Kendall and three friends.

I put a smile on my face, even though I had expected the room to pack out. *Hey,* I thought, *it's just the first minute and there are already three people, maybe more on their way.*

I waited another ten minutes, and no one else showed up. This was going to be it. But three new people? Had I not heard God after all? He had told me that the high schools of America were going to be saved, and three kids didn't look like America.

Lord, I said, *this isn't the dream I've been holding in my heart!*

I'm not sure I expected a response from Him. After all, He had not spoken to me since He had planted the dream in me at Spirit West Coast.

Then, in a sound more like a small explosion in my heart, I heard one word: *Preach!*

Preach? At a Jesus Club? I had figured I'd be talking with the kids, but preach? And to three people? Wouldn't it be better to go outside and try to round up more students?

Again I heard the word: *Preach!*

So I took a deep breath and that's what I did. I started to talk about Jesus and what He had done in my life. Within minutes Kendall and the three friends, who, I found out later, were not saved, were in tears. Following the example I had seen not long before when I had received Jesus at my church, I gave an altar call and asked if anyone in the room wanted to receive Jesus. Yes, I know. It was just as awkward as it sounds! I was twice as awkward saying it. But we prayed together and that day those three students found Jesus. I've learned that heaven rejoices the same whether one gets saved or thousands get saved.

It was a tiny start to the winning of American students for Jesus, but it was up to God to figure out how to make His plan work.

Over the next couple of months, word began to spread about the crazy guy in P6 talking about Jesus. The club grew slowly. Some weeks the whole classroom was full. Most of the kids who came were atheists or followers of various non-Christian faiths. I guess the lie that kids didn't want God wasn't true.

Week after week I went into the Bible Club and preached as though I had the attention of the whole campus. I stopped focusing on low numbers and started to speak as though I were talking to the entire school in the gym. Since I was not the greatest preacher and had no fancy equipment, the messages I gave were pretty raw with two key elements: the Bible and passion. But my faithfulness must have provoked God to move on our behalf. The students, though they came with curiosity, were generally polite. Few set out to challenge me or my message about Jesus.

As I was leaving one day, Mr. Schottle told me he would not be in school for the club meetings the next week. Since we could not meet in P6, he had arranged for us to use a room in the science building.

My first thought was that this would be perfect for inviting new students since it was near the quad, where many would be gathering over lunchtime. My second thought was that this was the classroom where I had failed science my sophomore year.

When I walked into the classroom the next Tuesday, the memories of the despair I had known at that time in my life walked in with me—the days I sat hopelessly in the very seats that were about to be occupied by students who might be feeling the same way. I remembered the countless times during my high school years that I actually wanted to take my life because I felt so empty and broken.

But here I was, eighteen years old now, a high school graduate and filled with hope for the ones who were about to sit in these chairs during lunch. I stared at the empty seats waiting for students to come and, I hoped, fill every one of them.

The bell rang and I shook off the daydreams. It was game time. Students started to come into the classroom—to my surprise, more than usual. I greeted them as they walked in, both new people and a few who had been coming regularly.

They sat down and, after Kendall introduced me, I prayed as I always did, "Jesus, encounter us. Amen."

I started to preach, telling stories of what God had done in my life and explaining how, since He had encountered me, I had never been the same. Their eyes were locked in. For most of these kids, it was their first time hearing the truth about Jesus. I had seen God do some amazing things with the handful of students who gathered every week—but that day something felt different. And what happened next would give me hope for students all across America.

About halfway through my message, the door opened and a small group of punk rockers filled the doorway. They scanned the room and walked casually to a few empty chairs, smiling at the small disruption their appearance was causing.

On one side of the room were the few Christian students, looking a little nervous. On the other side, looking dark and hostile in their black skinny jeans and earrings, were punk rockers who may never have seen the inside of a church in their lives.

I thought to myself, *God help me!*

This was the moment I had waited for. I longed for the lost to come and get saved—and here they were. But truth be told, I was terrified at what to do. The only thing I could figure, in the few seconds I had to think, was not to abandon the one directive I had been given by God: Preach. I hoped that if I finished preaching my message, God would do the rest.

So I kept on preaching. The punk rockers seemed to be listening to every word I spoke, but I was not able to tell if they were really connecting with what I was saying. I had the feeling they were waiting for me to say something they could use as a means to discredit me—or perhaps disprove God.

As I continued to speak and came close to wrapping up the meeting, something happened that I was not prepared for. God spoke to me in that very moment. He told me to stop my message and to start praying for the students out loud.

That didn't seem like a good idea. Some of these students had no concept of Jesus. If I started praying, what would they think? But His voice came to me strongly again to pray for them to be healed from depression and suicide and brokenness in Jesus' name. Again I thought about what they would say. And again the Lord spoke to me. I could no longer hold out against His words. I knew I had to act now, even though I had no understanding of what was going on.

So I stopped talking. All eyes were on me, including those of the teacher who was taking Mr. Schottle's place that day.

Then I told them, "This might be weird, but I am going to pray for you guys."

I said it so fast that no one had a chance to oppose it. I closed my eyes and started praying with everything I had. What started off as a weak prayer turned into a bold declaration.

"Jesus, You know every heart in this room. You know the lives these students have had, the suicidal thoughts, the addictions and their brokenness. Jesus, heal them."

I was a little shocked at what I was asking, but on I went. "Jesus, touch their hearts and lives, just as You have touched mine."

As words flowed out, God started to move. I could hear the reactions of the students as sniffles turned into weeping, and then sobs. I opened my eyes slowly, and to my amazement I saw one of the punk rocker girls, dressed in black and looking depressed, getting touched by God. Though I had not paid much attention to her specifically when the group came in, I did remember the look of sadness on her face as she took her seat. I had no clue what she was going through, but I could tell she needed hope desperately.

As I continued to pray, she fell to her knees and began to weep more loudly. The atmosphere in the room was shifting. The focus was no longer on whether or not God was real; the challenge now was whether or not these students would accept Jesus into their hearts.

I asked if anyone wanted to receive Jesus. Hands went up everywhere. The punk rockers all raised their hands.

I led them in a prayer to ask Jesus into their hearts, knowing the bell would ring any minute.

As we finished and the kids began leaving for their classes, the depressed girl who had been weeping came up to me and told me her name was Crystal.

"My friends and I heard about you," she said, "and we came today to challenge you. But I've never felt anything like the feeling I got when you prayed."

Then, through fresh tears, she started pouring out all the pain in her life. My heart broke over how much the devil had lied to her. *But* God had done a work in her life in one minute. Crystal had met the Jesus of love and compassion. He was now her Lord and Savior, and He had started to take away the scars on her heart.

Every single time I saw Crystal that year—she was usually smiling and talking with someone about Jesus—I was reminded of the woman in Luke 7:47 whose sins were forgiven and who carried such gratitude. Crystal was grateful that God had set her free, and she was a sign and a wonder of what God had done in this Jesus Club.

I guess you could say that God used my willing yes to change kids like Crystal, but honestly, their saying yes to God changed my own life as well. I began to see the eagerness in the students at Elk Grove High to know this Man named Jesus.

There were many stories like Crystal's throughout that first year. There was the popular football player, who happened to come into the room one day and got touched by God. There was the atheist who in one moment received Jesus because he felt the Lord's tangible touch. There was the girl who got delivered from demonic oppression after years of being tormented in her dreams. There were the security guards whose lives were touched by simple prayers we said with them in the quad. There was the young Hindu girl, who after hearing the message of Jesus gave her life to Christ and professed Jesus to her family.

But I'm getting ahead of my story.

When I got home the day we met in the science room, the day Crystal and the others came to Jesus, everything felt unreal, yet very real—if that makes sense. Jesus had invaded that campus and touched the lives of many Elk Grove High students. I was incredibly thankful for the work He was doing, but questions remained.

He had told me He wanted to release a movement that would take the high schools of America. I had seen the rewards of obedience in the lives of a handful of students. I knew in my heart that God wanted to invade all the campuses across the nation. He wanted to pour His love over every student. And His lovingkindness, I knew, would lead them to repentance.

But the question remained: How would every high school student hear about Jesus?

3

THE JESUS RALLIES

N JESUS' NAME, AMEN!"
I had finished preaching a little early to the twenty or so students at the Jesus Club meeting that lunchtime. It was a chilly November afternoon, only about two months since I had first talked with Mr. Schottle and Kendall. I was about to suggest something that would take every ounce of faith in me to see come to pass.

I met with the club twice every week, and God was doing an amazing work there. We never had packed rooms, but new students came every week. As the kids chatted and finished their lunches, I was struck with an idea. I interrupted them a little abruptly.

"Hey, you guys?"

Heads turned in my direction.

"I was just remembering the black light rallies we used to have in the gym when I went to school here. Do you still have those?"

Heads nodded yes, so I kept going.

"And at those rallies there is music and lights and they are really fun and the whole school shows up, right?"

Again heads bobbed, but the expressions were looking more and more puzzled.

Realizing they were not sure where I was going, I spelled it out. "What if we had a *Jesus* rally? What if our little Jesus Club had a massive impact on the whole school?"

Their faces were priceless as their eyes lit up; to be truthful I was shocked at what was coming out of my mouth. They had probably never thought anything like this could come from their Jesus Club—and neither had I.

Inspired by the fact that at least they were not saying no, I charged ahead.

"What if hundreds gathered in the theater after school and we preached about Jesus—and they all came to know Him? What if our Jesus Rally was better than any kind of rally the school has ever put on?"

In that moment I realized this was not my idea or a good idea: It was a *God* idea. But as I kept talking, negative thoughts crept into my mind: *What are you saying? Are you crazy? You can't do something like this!*

In that sense, the voice was right. I could not do something like this. Mr. Schottle and Kendall and the great kids in the club could not do this. But I had begun my journey with the belief that this generation has heard enough of people saying what God cannot do. I wanted them to understand the possibility of what He *can* do.

And these kids were ready to be challenged. They smiled as faith filled their hearts, too. Our ideas for a rally began popping.

"We can have music—"

"—a Christian band. Maybe a hip-hop artist!"

"We can get somebody to work the lights. . . ."

"We'll need a lot of free food. . . ."

"We can bring our friends and give flyers to every student on campus. . . ."

The more the conversation buzzed around the room the more it took hold. I think the creativity for ideas like this was in their hearts all the time, but no one had ever given them permission to dream for something they could not do on their own—something so big that God would have to do it.

I looked at Kendall, who grinned back at me, and we both turned almost in unison toward Mr. Schottle. He was sitting in his chair with a nervous look on his face.

I held my breath waiting to see what God would do. This was a crucial moment. If we began exploring everything that could go wrong, we would quickly quench our faith. But if we let our faith fly—and mixed it with excitement—we could believe in the possibility of all that could go *right*!

"Well," he began slowly, and then I saw this side smile I would come to recognize when I said something he liked or had a crazy idea. "Well," he said again, "nobody has ever done such a thing, but I suppose it can be done."

I was stoked that he went for it. Mr. Schottle pulled open his desk drawer and took out his calendar. The only possible date was Monday, December 14, 2009. In our enthusiasm we determined that this gave us plenty of time to prepare for a Jesus Rally. Kendall asked Mr. Schottle if he would go to bat for us and get us access to the theater.

He said yes, and it was official.

Well, at least in our minds and hearts it was official. We had many logistics to maneuver but that seemed to us like a minor concern. What really mattered was our willingness to risk.

It was clear that we were in over our heads, but I wanted the kids to understand that our job is simply to be obedient—to do our best with whatever God asks of us. If we could get students to a rally, and lift Jesus up, He would draw them to Himself. Either God would show up or we would look like fools. The decision was His. But either way I knew I would rather look like a fool than risk someone not coming to Jesus because I was afraid to hurt my reputation.

As if on cue, the bell rang. And as we did every week, the students and I walked out of the classroom and joined the other students on campus—students who had no idea what we had just dreamed about in that room. I walked with mixed emotions through the blue gates toward the parking lot, taking a moment for my weekly routine of handshakes and small talk with the security guards.

I got into my car, but before I put the key into the ignition, it hit me: I had no money and no planning skills to pull this off. I drove home slowly, wanting to keep my eyes on the wonderful dream that had been birthed in the classroom but sensing small fears starting to crowd around and block it from view.

Once home, I began to plan as best as I could, adding up the potential cost on my phone calculator. Over the next couple of weeks, Kendall and I met with Mr. Schottle, who confirmed that the theater was reserved. After hours of talking and calculating and trying to keep the costs down, it looked as though we would need a thousand dollars. This would cover the food, lighting, sound system, expenses for the guest speaker and musicians, and a few other things.

That might not sound like a big amount, but to a kid with no paying job this was the most money I could almost imagine. I knew from the first day I set foot on the school grounds that I would never charge a student a dime. I knew that God had called me to go and preach, so any cost that came with that call was mine to cover. I also never wanted anyone to say we took anything from any student. On the contrary I wanted them to say we gave it all. I did my best never to show my fears about money to the Jesus Club. I somehow was sure that the money would come in one way or another.

Soon we found ourselves passing out two thousand flyers on campus—the flyers were donated to us—and we could feel the momentum growing. Every week as I walked to P6 I overheard students talking about the rally. It was too late to back out now.

One day at the Jesus Club I talked openly about the money we needed so they would pray with me for Jesus to respond. Almost instinctively the kids reached for their backpacks. I was speechless as they drew out their wallets and offered me the few bills they had.

With a quick prayer for guidance, I told them to keep their money but asked that they pray. I knew a little about "sowing seeds," meaning giving what you have for a venture you believe in, but in this case I truly believed that their willingness to give was enough to move God's heart.

So we stood and gathered together to pray, asking God to show up and do what only He could do. At one point, I opened my eyes and looked around at the heads bowed in fervent prayer. Just three months prior, Kendall, Mr. Schottle and I had joined together to put ourselves at God's disposal through the Jesus Club. Now we were going after the salvation of students who might never come to a weekly meeting in a classroom but would come to a rally.

After our meeting, I left and passed the theater on my right where the rally would be held. I wondered if the door was unlocked—and was surprised to find that it was. I peeked in, found it empty and slipped inside.

In the quiet of the room I began to pray, asking God to fill it for the Jesus Rally. With tears in my eyes, I prayed with all of my heart that God would provide the money we needed and bring the students. I wanted desperately to see souls saved. In that moment I was reminded of the Spirit West Coast gathering where God told me He was going to save the high schools of America.

Well, I thought, *moving from a classroom to a theater is a start!*

I left quietly trying not to call attention to myself, since I did not have permission to be in there.

Another week went by. We were now one week away from the rally and I was beginning to worry.

"Lord," I prayed, "You want to save these students. I ask You to provide everything we need to reach them. We can't do this without You. You have to come through!" That was my prayer. That Tuesday morning, as I was on my way to Elk Grove High, I said to God, "If You don't give me the money, I quit. There's no way we can do this without You." I felt a little like Moses when he told God he could not go on without His presence.

This was not an arrogant prayer but a desperate one. I never wanted to do anything that Jesus was not backing. When I had first spoken of this rally to the Jesus Club, I truly believed that God was inspiring my words. Now we needed that inspiration to be confirmed by His backing.

After preaching that day I drove to my church, where I spent most of my time. As I pulled into the parking lot, feeling down, I was met by my youth pastor, who told me that people from the church had heard what we were trying to do and had donated some money.

Was this God's answer? I asked him how much and was thrilled when he said eight hundred dollars.

I thanked him and thought, *We are almost there!*

Now we needed just two hundred dollars more.

When I spent time with the Lord in prayer that evening, I was super grateful and super expectant that He was hearing me—and that maybe we would not have to cancel this Jesus Rally.

I prayed with an odd mix of heaviness and joy, both leading me to pray with more fervor. I closed my eyes and went to bed that night with a smile, feeling certain God would complete what He had started.

After I finished preaching the following day, I told the students about the eight hundred dollars. They rejoiced with me, happy and excited about what God was doing.

On my way back to church from the Jesus Club, I was tired and thirsty. I took a different turn from my normal route, planning to swing by a place called Jamba Juice to get my favorite smoothie. As I drove past the familiar sites—the burrito shop, the tire shop, the creek to my left that I used to walk past every day on my way to school—I began to wonder what I would have done differently had I known then what I knew now.

At least now I could make a difference.

I was on Elk Grove Boulevard—if you have been on this road you know how it seems to go on forever, especially with traffic—when I passed it: a skateboard shop. I had seen this place many times before but had never gone in since I am not a skater. All of a sudden the same voice I had heard at camp spoke clearly again.

Go to the skateboard shop.

Hesitant, because I figured I was hearing things and was eager to get my smoothie and get to the church to pray, I kept driving. Plus, I wondered how that thought could be from God. There was nothing spiritual about it.

Go to the skateboard shop.

"No," I said out loud, a little upset at not understanding what I was hearing.

Go to the skateboard shop.

I heard it again, but this time I knew it was God. Still I argued.

"God," I said, "I'm tired and I want to get something to drink. And this doesn't even make sense! Why are You asking me to go to a skate shop when I don't even skate? Anyway, I have to find two hundred dollars. I just need some time to clear my head and think and pray."

God said for the fourth time, *Brian, I want you to go to that skateboard shop.*

I could no longer ignore what the Lord was telling me, even though it made absolutely no sense. He didn't tell me why I had to go, only that I had to go, and that I had to go now.

I finally gave in. What did I have to lose?

I wish I could say that I had joy in obeying this random request from the Lord, but I did not. Flipping an illegal U-turn, I headed back a short way and turned into the parking lot, pulling to a stop at the farthest space available. I figured that just in case this turned out to be awkward, I could get back into my car and not be noticed. I got out of the car and walked toward the shop.

As the squeaky glass door closed behind me, I glanced around wondering what to do. I have to say I was impressed with the cool things in the store. The woman behind the cash register saw me come in and had that look on her face people get when they are expecting you to start a conversation.

I walked toward her and was surprised to recognize her. I had met her and her husband once while standing in line for a ride at Six Flags Marine World, a theme park in Southern California. I remembered that they owned a skate shop but could not believe it was this one. They were Christians and attended a church nearby. But still this whole situation made no sense to me.

"Hello," I said. "How are you? Do you remember me?"

She did indeed remember me and greeted me warmly. Thinking to myself that this conversation had nowhere else to go, I started telling her what God was speaking to me about the high schools of America. I described the students who were getting saved on the campus, wonderful kids like Crystal.

From this woman's big smile and nods, I was encouraged to go on talking. She looked excited by what I was saying. I felt happy that her heart was stirred as much as mine. And I really didn't know what else to talk about.

Eventually I got to the dream we had for the Jesus Rally. I mean, what the heck? I figured I might as well go all out. So I told her about the possibility of hundreds of students getting saved who would never come to the Jesus Club.

Her eyes began to get big, and I knew at that moment I had heard God correctly about going to the skate shop. Finally I shared with her the miracle of eight hundred dollars coming in at practically the last minute but how we needed two hundred more.

She raised her hand to stop me, and her eyes filled with tears.

"Young man," she said, "as I was getting ready for work this morning, the Holy Spirit told me to bring two hundred dollars with me. He told me that someone would come into the shop today who needs it."

"What!" I said.

My heart instantly dropped with regret over my argument with the Lord earlier.

She reached down under the counter for her purse, took out her wallet and pulled out two one-hundred-dollar bills.

"This is your money," she said, handing me the cash.

Tears started to fill my eyes.

What if I had kept driving? What if I had given up? It was my first test and reward of blind obedience.

I took the money, looked at her and said, "Thank you so much. You have no idea what this means!"

Her faith and obedience in giving did more for me than she will ever know. It taught me at a young age in the Lord that God doesn't have to give you details, only direction. Then I told her the story of my car ride to her shop, and we both understood that as we obeyed, God answered.

I thanked her over and over again. And that was not the end of her generosity. She donated skateboards to give away at the event, and said that she and her husband would be there.

As I walked to my car and slipped into the seat, I was in total awe and amazement of God. This Jesus Rally truly was heaven's idea. God had backed it in ways I would have never thought possible.

"Jesus," I said out loud, "I'm so sorry. Please forgive my attitude and my thoughts."

With a thankful heart, I drove out of the parking lot, eager to get to church and finish planning. We had the money. This event was going to happen. I figured that the students and my family wouldn't believe this story if I told them!

That trip to the skateboard shop was a faith-changer for me. At that moment, I knew I would be safe to trust God's every word. I knew that no matter what wild things He might ask me to do in the future, it would be okay. He would provide for me and for whatever dream He gave me.

In fact, I didn't know it then, but there would be days when people would share their own dreams with me—and sometimes they would shake their heads and say that the funds never came in or things fell short. Yet if I am to be honest, I have only known a Jesus who provides everything. That lesson in blind obedience convinced me that He will fulfill whatever He asks me to do. A man told me once that God has a special place in His heart for ministries that win souls. I can truly believe that.

But driving back along Elk Grove Boulevard toward church that day, my smoothie in hand, I was not thinking any further into the future than His plans for the Jesus Rally less than a week away.

With every day that passed, I felt more and more eager for Sunday to come. The janitors, who had become friends over the previous months, were going to let us in early so we could spend Sunday setting up for the rally Monday afternoon.

At last the day came. Our small Jesus Club team was arriving to get the theater ready.

It felt surreal.

As we brought in the speakers and lights and picked up trash inside of the theater, I had time to think about our excitement in the classroom as we talked about this day. And how my walk with God had changed. I had learned not only to hear God's voice and obey, but also to do things simply because I know it's His heart.

What do I mean by this? Jesus told us to go and make disciples, right? And disciples are made by hearing the Gospel. And they hear the Gospel by someone speaking. So we don't have to wake up every day and ask Jesus if we should tell people about Him. We just go ahead and do it because it's His heart. I was learning to risk it all, even if it meant looking foolish for the dream God had given me.

When I woke up early the next day for the Jesus Rally, I sought the Lord in prayer, asking that this be not just an event but an encounter for these students. The number of kids who would attend was still unknown. We had passed out many flyers and there was a buzz on campus about it, but nothing like this had ever taken place there so we had nothing to compare it to.

I got to the theater well ahead of time, my heart racing with anticipation. Back and forth I paced, making sure everything was ready. The lights and sound were on point. The Jesus Club students had permission to leave their last classes a little early, and of course that made them happy.

Then at 3:13 p.m., the bell rang. The school day was over.

We pushed open the theater doors and started playing some of my favorite songs from Lecrae, a hip-hop artist who loves Jesus. At almost the same moment, we dimmed the lights and turned the strobes on, which made the theater look like a nightclub.

I stood outside the doors inviting people in. One, then two, then three and four—and pretty soon kids were walking through the doors in groups.

I could not believe it. They were actually coming!

The two hundred seats were filled quickly, and other kids who had come a little late were filling the foyer behind the theater doors.

"It is time to start, Brian!" Kendall shouted over the music. "Here's the mic."

I made my way quickly to the front and climbed the steps to the stage. I was used to speaking to a handful of students at the Jesus Club every week in Mr. Schottle's room, but never anything like this. I certainly had never spoken to this many students who were probably mostly unsaved. But my excitement over the Jesus Rally took care of my nervousness.

Someone turned down the music, and I stared at the room full of people who were now looking back at me. I welcomed them, trying to keep calm, but feeling completely crazy inside.

I kept thinking, *God, You really did it! And You're about to save all of these students.* To me it wasn't a matter of *if* but of *when*, and that *when* was *now*.

I knew in my heart this was the first time 95 percent of these students were hearing music about Jesus, but as the band named "Called to Arms" began performing, the kids went wild with excitement, clapping and moving to the beats, not knowing that in just a few minutes the words they were dancing to would have real meaning in their lives. They would be offered the opportunity to step from darkness into light.

After a number of songs, the band finished, and I went to the front of the stage once again.

"Okay," I said into the mic. "Everyone grab your seat. We have one more amazing thing before we let you all go and get your free food." Students shouted at that statement of free food. I knew most of them had come for that very reason—but they were about to leave with something more.

As they settled into their seats, I said, "Can you welcome up our speaker as he shares a message I believe will change your life?"

Our speaker, a local youth pastor I was friends with, stood and walked to the front of the stage. The room grew quiet. Every eye was fixed on him and what was about to happen next. He began to speak about Jesus.

For my part, honestly, I sat there hoping the students wouldn't leave. They *had* to stay and hear this part—this was what it was all about. As the speaker poured out truth about Christ and the cross and what Jesus did for their lives, I watched as the kids' faces began to reflect their hearts. Everything started to change. Most of them had never heard the Gospel in their lives. And they probably never thought they would first hear it in their high school theater.

The moment of truth came.

"How many in this room want to receive Jesus into your hearts?" he asked.

It felt as though the room stood still.

And then God walked in.

"If that's you today, and you want to know and accept and receive Him, will you stand to your feet?"

The silence was quickly overcome by the sound of shuffling feet and the theater's folding chair seats flipping shut. I watched from backstage as two hundred students stood to meet Jesus.

My eyes filled instantly with tears, and again I was reminded of what the Lord had told me—that He was going to save the high schools of America.

With one voice, the students followed the words of the speaker, proclaiming loudly their public confession of Christ. I felt certain that this was a sound that had never been heard in the history of that school. I wish I could have seen what happened in the Spirit that day as two hundred students gave their lives to Jesus.

With the chorus of "Amen!" I saw tears in the eyes of many. They might have walked in dead, but they were leaving alive.

As the kids made their way to the food tables, talking and laughing with one another, I stood there amazed. I could imagine that their thoughts of Jesus being uncool had been completely thrown out—but not by our lights or sound or food. It was by our boldness to be unashamed, to be willing to look like fools if that was what it took.

Not only was the Jesus Rally the rally of the year, but it had purpose and meaning, and that was something rare for these kids who had been mostly walking down dead-end roads.

As they left the theater that afternoon, the Jesus Club leaders and I said good-bye and wondered what God would do next. The word God had spoken to me of His plan to save the high schools of America was becoming a little clearer. Still not in full picture but definitely clearer.

I was beginning to understand that the real issue in my generation is not rejection of the Gospel: When given the opportunity to receive Jesus, these students had responded quickly—as though they had been waiting all their lives. The real problem is that most students have never seen Jesus or seen many people who look, act, walk and talk like Him. God was showing me that when kids see Jesus in our lives, they will realize how much they want to know Him.

The next day came fast. I no longer walked unnoticed as I headed to Jesus Club for our Tuesday meeting. I was greeted by many students who had been at the Jesus Rally or who had heard about it. The name of Jesus was starting to be made famous at Elk Grove High.

I continued week after week that school year, preaching more than sixty sermons about the Gospel in P6 and seeing Jesus touch many lives. Our Jesus Club was somewhat cramped in that classroom—sometimes as many as 35 students came—but we continued to meet there. Our message was simple: Jesus and giving our lives to Him, calling the students to follow after Him and His teachings.

We held one more Jesus Rally that year with the faith and hope that God would save even more students. We had a sense that the theater would not hold the numbers that we anticipated would come, so we reserved the gym.

You may or may not know that April 20 is a popular day with high school students. It's known as "National Pot Smoking Day." That was the day we chose to hold our second rally. We spread the word on campus that God was the "most high" and to come and try Jesus. I know it sounds like something borrowed from hippies in the 1960s, but it worked.

At that second Jesus Rally, more than six hundred students gathered in the gym and committed their lives to Jesus.

In all, eight hundred students came to know Jesus through those two Jesus Rallies. The rallies were not designed to motivate them to have a better life or to advertise a club. The rallies were an invitation to meet a Man who would change their lives forever.

Elk Grove High was never the same after that year. Yes, eight hundred was not America, but I honestly thought I had seen it all: a Jesus Club filling a classroom, hundreds filling the theater and gym for the rallies—what more could God do?

Little did I know that what I was about to see Jesus do on the campuses of Elk Grove would set the course of my life—and be the start of a new missions movement in America.

4

FROM SIX TO
SIX HUNDRED

AS THAT 2009-2010 SCHOOL YEAR finished, I was amazed at what God had done. Hundreds had met Jesus. Some of the Jesus Club students had graduated. Now a hot Elk Grove summer awaited me.

Toward the end of the school year, with a mix of emotions, I had begun pondering what was next. I did not sense that the Lord was directing me to preach only at Elk Grove High, but should I plan to preach at other schools? I truly did not know what to do. The only reason I was not thinking about college or pursuing a career was the voice I had heard in my heart saying the high schools of America would be saved. I knew that whatever He was asking would require my fully devoted attention and heart.

As summer came I started to read books on revival—and everything I read left me asking God, Why not again?

From stories of William J. Seymour and Azusa Street to Evan Roberts and the Welsh Revival, from evangelists like Smith Wigglesworth to others described in the well-known book *God's Generals*, I devoured the pages and words from these great people of faith, finding myself in a similar place. I was praying for high school students to encounter God just as they had prayed for their cities and countries to encounter God.

But even though my heart was encouraged at moments, I found myself at the uncomfortable crossroads between the words God had spoken and the social pressure that was building. After all I was about to turn twenty. Many of my friends were in college and had cars and serious relationships and—well, for me, I was what you would call a campus missionary, a term not as fully understood as it is now.

As I stood in my kitchen that summer day making a turkey and avocado sandwich, the thought of reaching students on every campus in America suddenly felt like a weight too heavy to bear. I started to consider every reason why God could not and should not use me.

I almost wanted Him to disqualify me, to release me from the task He had given me. Not that I didn't want to follow through or didn't love God, but the unknown was frightening. And although I had seen Him work and knew He would provide, the burden simply felt too great.

As these many thoughts flooded my mind, I reached the place where I could go no further. It was too much.

With every bit of strength left in me I slammed my hands on the counter and shouted at the top of my lungs: "God, I can't do this!"

I didn't care if anyone heard me. I was desperate for an answer. Tears began pouring from my eyes, running down my cheeks. My throat actually felt hoarse from yelling so loud.

I had no idea how to do what God had asked me to do—but I knew in my heart at that moment that the unknown was not the real problem. The weight of reaching students along with the social pressure coming at me was not the real problem either.

I had prayed to accept Jesus as Lord of my life, and the real problem was what it would cost. The cost was not money or even time; it was much more. It was my life; it was my will; it was my future being completely yielded to God, trusting Him fully. This was far riskier than giving my money or time. Money can be re-saved and time can be made up, but you can never get back your life. Once it is given, it doesn't belong to you anymore.

In the midst of my brokenness and weakness, I heard the Lord speak to me again.

With a tender voice of love He said, *Brian, I want you to go into Laguna Creek High School, and I will show you what I am about to release across the campuses of this nation.*

I froze, startled. This was not the response I had expected to hear. Now, I knew about Laguna. There were only nine high schools in the Elk Grove Unified School District at that time, and Laguna had a reputation for being a rough one.

I thought to myself, *Here I am, pouring out my deep concerns, giving my two-weeks' notice to God that I am quitting campus missions, and He completely ignores me.*

But I also realized He saw something in me that I could not see.

I stood there at the counter a few minutes longer, wondering why Laguna had anything to do with anything.

Then I made the decision that charted the course of the rest of my life.

I have obeyed this far, I thought, *and God has never let me down or left me out to dry.*

With the weakest yes I had ever uttered in my life, I told God, "I'll give it one more year."

As I wiped the tears from my eyes with the back of my hand, I was shocked to feel a quickening of faith rise in my heart.

In an instant, everything changed. I hoped now that no one had heard my cry of quitting! I was embarrassed by my unwillingness to carry out my assignment.

My heart was back to believing all that God had spoken to me the year before at Spirit West Coast. I sat down at the kitchen table with my sandwich and tried to think of any connection I had to Laguna Creek High School. Surprisingly I remembered one. A few months earlier I had met a girl from another church who was a student there. Her name was Lisa.

Things took off from there. After a few conversations with Lisa, who would be leading the Bible club at Laguna that year, with me possibly helping by preaching every week, we decided to go for it and dream for God to work on that campus. This time I didn't feel as though I was starting off from day one by myself. The faith this girl carried was special. She really loved her school, and to me that was the thing that turns the key in the lock of the door of massive salvation.

So on a hot August day, a Wednesday, with the harvest ready and ripe to hear the Gospel—that is, with school back in session—I pulled up to the Laguna campus in the blue '97 Honda Accord that my Aunt Belinda had donated to me. I had the same mix of nervousness and expectation as I had experienced the first day at Elk Grove High the year before.

I took a deep breath, got out of the car and headed to the front office to sign in. The unfamiliar school grounds and new faces of teachers and administrators did little to soothe my emotions.

"Hello. May I help you?" As the front door slammed behind me, the woman at the front desk looked at me curiously.

"Yes," I said, trying to sound confident. "I'm going to the Bible club today and wanted to know what room it'll be in."

"Yes," she said. "That would be with Mr. Eric Johnson in P5. I'll write you a pass."

I'm in! I thought. That was a lot easier than I had imagined.

"Thanks," I said, and walked out the metal door she had pointed toward and went into an empty quad. The open quad, where students would hang out during lunch, seemed to echo silence, much like the calm before the storm.

Crossing the lawn and passing lockers, I headed to the very back of the campus. I was beginning to think that all great moves of God start in a small classroom that no one can find.

I did find it, though, and walked up the wooden ramp to P5. Then I waited outside for the bell that would signal the start of lunch. As soon as it rang, my hand went for the doorknob to open it and let myself in. Instead, the door was flung open to release a stampede of students, pouring out as if the building were on fire.

I waited till they all cleared the doorway, and then slowly stuck my head in.

"Hello? Mr. Johnson?" I said looking up to a man who was at least six foot three with a smile that broke all my fear of being there.

"Hi," he said. "My name is Mr. Johnson."

I stepped through the doorway.

"Hey, I'm Brian Barcelona," I said, extending my hand, "and I'm here to work with Lisa and the Bible club."

We talked only a moment about what was happening at Elk Grove High when Lisa walked in. I was happy to see her—as well as her five friends with her.

I had thought that introductory meeting might be filled with prayer and preaching, but that wasn't the case. We all sat in a circle, sharing our hearts for reaching the campus. When Lisa gave me the floor, I told them about God's words to me and what He had done at Elk Grove High through the Jesus Club. As I talked, I began to see faith rise in the small group of students.

I realized the importance of seizing that moment and asked this question: "What do you think God can do in this campus?"

Now, I was used to hearing things like, "He can help me get an *A* on my test" or "He can make my teachers not so annoying." So, truth be told, I wasn't ready to hear what came out of Lisa's mouth.

"I believe God can save my school," she said.

She spoke with so much confidence and assurance that the idea of her whole school being saved seemed like a reality.

My heart leaped with joy. I mean, I had never seen a campus saved, but here was actually a student who believed that God could do it.

I was quick to respond.

"Well," I said, "if you believe that, then I will believe with you."

Why I said what I said next I have no idea, but it opened the door for us to do nothing but trust God.

"Get me the theater during lunch," I said.

I knew there was a theater because I had passed it in the quad. I had no idea how many it held, but if it was like Elk Grove's then we could get at least a few hundred inside.

"The theater will seat five hundred, tops," Lisa said thoughtfully, explaining that the theater had 250 seats and could be used for both lunches since the school had so many kids.

Then she added, "We only have six students here!"

I nodded and then said, "If you get it, God will fill it."

The room stood silent, but I knew it was the silence of pondering—pondering what was possible. Then it was as though we all chose to make a vow together. The vow was this: We wanted God to move on this campus, and risk was our only option. We could play it safe and stay in P5, but if we wanted God to reach the students, we had to provide room for them to fit in so they could hear His Good News.

If we were going to pray for God to do something, then we needed to act as though we believed He would actually do it.

The meeting ended shortly after this. Six students and I now had a plan. But once again the only one who could make this happen was God. It would take us another week to book the theater for our regular club meetings, so we decided to hold one more meeting in P5.

When the next Wednesday came, we didn't know if any more students would show up or if it would be the same six again. Lisa had invited all of her friends and so did the others. It was D-Day for us—our first Jesus Club.

I got there extra early—about an hour early, to be exact—and again got out of my '97 Honda and walked toward the main door. This time the campus wasn't so intimidating. I went through that now-familiar door and greeted the woman at the front desk with a smile, letting her know why I was there and getting my pass, which became my routine as I preached at that school for the next two and a half years.

I then headed to the classroom and, this time, knew to wait for the students to pile out. As soon as the bell rang and they charged past me, I went in and greeted Mr. Johnson—whom the students called "Mr. J."

I got ready, opened my Bible and waited.

That day sixty students came to the club.

I had never seen anything like this. Though hundreds had come to the Jesus Rallies at Elk Grove High, it had taken a year to build the club membership to 35 students. Something was different about this school. The students' hunger to check out who Jesus was seemed to me something rare.

I preached that day with great enthusiasm about Zacchaeus coming down from the tree, and how we need to do the same sometimes to get to Jesus. As I finished, I prayed and then greeted the new students.

One in particular stood out to me. I could tell this guy was a leader by the way he carried himself and how those around him respected him. His name was Don. I went over to say hello.

"Hey, man," I said, "did you enjoy today?"

"You're crazy, man!" he said with a smile. I knew he was talking about how passionately I preached.

"Am I? Who's crazier, me or the one listening to me?" We both laughed.

"You didn't leave," I continued, "so there must be something you liked, right?"

He agreed.

"Will I see you next week in the theater for the Jesus Club?" I asked.

"I'll be there," he said.

I shook his hand, and he and some of his friends headed out the door.

Don Jackson, who turned out to be the captain of the football team, gave his life to Jesus that year, along with most of the teammates he had brought along.

Right before he left high school, I told him, laughing, "One day you're going to go to the NFL, and when you do, I want field tickets." I sensed that God had a wild plan for this man's life.

As of this writing, Don is playing for the Green Bay Packers. He mentioned to me not long ago that the Jesus Club changed his life.

What a day that was for the first Jesus Club meeting at Laguna Creek High School! We all said afterward that no more kids could have fit in P5 if we had tried. Now the moment of truth was about to come. Would we see even more in the theater? That whole next week we all prayed—me, the six student leaders and Mr. J.—for God to do something extraordinary.

I showed up that next Wednesday an hour early with fifteen boxes of pizza I had bought with money that a few people had donated. This time while the secretary was writing my pass, I told her I would not be in P5 today but would be in the theater. With a curious smile she handed me my pass.

I made my way to the theater, balancing pizza boxes in my arms—having left the rest at the front desk so I wouldn't drop any. No one was allowed to eat in the theater, so we planned to hand out slices to the kids after the meeting. I thought to myself how Jesus gave fish; we would give pizza. Same concept; different generation.

Two weeks had passed since I had made the bold statement that God would fill the theater. And now my words would be tested.

Even if just those sixty come back, I'll be happy, I said, trying not to get my hopes too high.

The bell for first lunch rang and I stood waiting right by the theater doors. I figured this was the best spot for inviting kids in, as the entrance and exit both faced the quad where hundreds of students gathered at lunchtime. The first to arrive were the six Jesus Club student leaders. Then more students started coming into the room and filling the seats. I could hardly believe my eyes. *How did so many students hear about this?* I wondered. Two hundred came that day, to be exact, one hundred for the first lunch and one hundred for the second lunch.

Standing there before both groups with a mic in my hand, faith in my heart and an audience I could never have imagined, I began to preach the Gospel. My job was to stand there and talk. God's job was to touch their hearts.

"It is love that God has for us, and it's not like any love you have ever encountered," I shouted, growing more passionate as the words poured out of my mouth.

As I made the call during those two lunchtimes that September day for students to receive Jesus, I was overwhelmed at the response. All two hundred students stood to their feet with tears filling their eyes. More tears began to fill mine at the amazing sight of this many kids receiving Jesus at just a regular Jesus Club meeting. And only months before I was about to quit! My weak yes made a major difference in these students' lives. As I finished speaking, I said that I would see them the next week.

As the second group cleared the theater, the six Jesus Club leaders and Mr. Johnson and I stood together in awe. We knew this was not normal—and it was only the beginning. We talked for only a short time because the students and Mr. J. had to get back to class.

I was thinking that this was the best it could ever get. But I had underestimated God. In a few more weeks this Jesus Club would make history in our city and become a story that would encourage people all across America to believe God is not finished with our high schools.

That week I did nothing but tell everyone I met what I had seen God do. And how we were trusting that God would do even more.

The next Wednesday, I showed up at the theater as promised with another message I had gotten in prayer. The bell rang and we again opened the theater doors to hundreds of students. Three hundred came this time, 150 in each lunch. We could hardly believe that the club was growing this fast. And the most amazing part was that 90 percent of the students coming were not Christians. The Jesus Club was getting the message of Jesus to students and bringing dead lives to life.

I gave a call for people to receive Jesus, and the kids who came with friends who had gotten saved the previous week also got saved.

And it didn't stop there.

The next week four hundred came, and the week after that, five hundred came. And I will never forget the day when someone said to me, "Brian, every seat is filled, and there are about eighty standing in the doorway."

In less than two months the Jesus Club had grown to nearly six hundred students coming every week. From drug dealers to straight-A students to popular athletes to atheists to homosexuals, the club welcomed everyone to come and hear about Jesus. Even gang members were attending. Sometimes I would hear them saying to one another, "You all ready for church today?" We knew once students could taste and see that the Lord is good, they would never go back to life without Him. Every week we heard stories of people turning to a new life in Christ.

And with the football team and the basketball team and the cheerleaders coming, the Jesus Club was the place to be during lunch on Wednesday.

Every week seemed to be more powerful than the one before. It wasn't long until word about Jesus Club spread to almost every student. Kids were surrendering their lives by the hundreds on the Laguna Creek High campus.

Although only six hundred could fit in the theater at one time, many more attended Jesus Club meetings, hearing the Gospel and giving their lives to Him. One-third of that campus got saved that year. A poll showed that 62 percent of the seniors alone had attended the Jesus Club at least once. This showed us that Jesus truly was drawing students to Himself.

The administration was extremely supportive of what God was doing since so many students were changing their behavior. It's not that we have bad kids, I would tell them, but we have broken ones. They need the Healer.

Every week it seemed that God had something different He wanted to say. Finding a message from the Bible was never hard for me since it felt as though God had waited fifteen, sixteen, seventeen years to speak to some of these students. For most of them, it was the first time in their lives they had heard the Gospel—and they were open to it. And their openness was fertile soil for truth and love to take root and lead to a life walking with Jesus.

That school year changed many lives, and I realized that one of those lives it had changed the most was mine. I never left a meeting without being amazed at God and what He was doing. God had once again proved His unfailing faithfulness.

My eyes were now fixed on the high school campuses of my city. And nothing could change my faith in believing that Jesus would save those students.

5

SET ME FREE

EVERY DAY THAT FALL I ASKED GOD TO show me how to share the Gospel at Laguna Creek High and Elk Grove High. I continued listening in my heart for His direction outward from there. The old wireless mics from the schools became my best friends as I preached to the students about God's love.

Whenever anyone asked me why I focused so much on God's love, I responded simply with this: Most students, if they even believe in a God, think that He wants nothing to do with them—that He is angry or mad at them. I wouldn't go as far as to say it is because their earthly fathers gave them a bad view of their heavenly Father, but I would say they cannot comprehend a God who has never been modeled for them.

As I prayed about the sermon I was about to preach in the Laguna Jesus Club meeting one particular week, I got insight that the best way to explain the condition those kids were in was not so much with words but with demonstration. Many of the students would be attending the club for the first time. Many others might have been coming for a month or so, but still the enemy was keeping them bound in some ways or they were having a hard time shaking their old lifestyles.

So that day, as I took the stage in front of hundreds of freshmen, sophomores, juniors and seniors to talk about the invisible chains that were binding them, I had the Jesus Club student leaders begin to wrap old rusty chains around me. The students who were watching this had confused looks on their faces, wondering what was going on. My passion and voice didn't tone down one bit as I began to tell them about freedom in Jesus while more and more chains restricted my freedom.

I knew from Scripture—in Romans 2:4—that God's lovingkindness leads us to repentance, and that's what began happening. Every student in the room had his or her eyes fixed on what was taking place. It was almost as though something supernatural was captivating each one. Because it truly is a sign and a wonder to get the attention of students these days, I knew, as the words flowed out of my mouth with clarity, that the message had not been birthed in my own skill but in the place of prayer. I sensed the hearts of the students in that theater beginning to soften. The Gospel reached more than just their minds; it reached the core of their being.

I gripped the mic ever tighter with sweaty palms, and I spoke with compassion that came from knowing I might not have tomorrow with these kids; I might not even have later. I had today. I had now. I could not let any one of them sit in hell today because I thought I had tomorrow to reach them.

From all my reading that summer, many things had stayed with me—particularly the words of Leonard Ravenhill, an English evangelist. He said, "A sermon born in the mind will reach the mind, but a sermon born in the heart through prayer will reach the heart."

This message of being chained had actually been burning in my heart for a long time after God had spoken to me that He wanted to save every high school in America. And my own memory of being bound in high school fueled the boldness to keep sharing the hope that I had now found.

With every word that came out of my mouth, something interesting began to happen. It felt as though the chains holding the students, chains that I felt as I preached, got heavier on me with each step closer to freedom they took.

Soon I was bound so tightly I could no longer move around; I could only stand in that one spot and use the one part of my body that would work: my voice. In that moment I felt that I connected with the students, much like Peter when he connected with the three thousand that got saved as he preached at Pentecost. It's one thing to speak a sermon; it's another to connect with those you are speaking to.

The lunchtime bell would ring soon. I felt the seconds ticking by, and these students needed to encounter God.

It was all or nothing. And now or never.

"Many in this room," I shouted, "have been bound to drugs, sex, gangs, hopelessness, abuse, addiction."

With so much conviction in my heart, I felt as though God had literally walked into that room. They must have felt Him, too, because tears streamed down many of their faces as the reality hit them. It was as though, once more, a veil was being torn, only this time it was the veil covering their eyes. The light of truth was breaking through the lies they had believed. In the presence of the God of love, the pain they had stuffed down and the abuse they had ignored could no longer hide—because darkness truly cannot remain where light is.

As I looked around the room, I could see God beginning to restore the innocence that had been robbed from many of them. Innocence that had been taken from their childhoods, taken by people who were meant to protect them.

I stopped speaking and silence filled the theater. I realized that we had moved past having a "good meeting." The Spirit of God had entered that room, and there was no escaping Him.

I could not tell if the kids knew exactly what they were feeling, but their faces spoke clearly. It looked like the same moment in my life three years earlier when I was sixteen and felt that same love grip my heart. It separated religion from relationship.

No longer were these students hearing about a God out there somewhere. No longer were they hoping that He loved them or questioning if He even existed. They were having an encounter that would forever change their lives.

Standing perfectly still with chains wrapped around my body, I was past fearing people's opinions.

"Listen!" I shouted into the mic. "I have these chains wrapped around me. I know I probably look crazy, but this is how you look spiritually."

Although it was a bold statement, I felt that I had to keep it real. In a generation where the prophets of kids' lives are the latest singers and rappers and TV actors, this was an Elijah moment of confronting every other voice. Every eye was locked onto me. I could sense that they saw not only the chains around me but those around themselves. What happened next would give me faith for the rest of my life to keep preaching on campuses and never give up on this mission field.

I kept shouting with all my being. "You may have walked into this theater today with chains wrapped around your heart. You may have walked into this room today enslaved by hurt, anger, unforgiveness, bitterness, resentment, self-hatred and lust, but these chains can't hold you anymore.

"It's an injustice to be bound when the price of freedom was already paid on the cross. The One who was perfect bore imperfection so that forever we can be perfect.

"It is for the sake of freedom that Jesus Christ set us free," I shouted, quoting from Galatians 5:1. "The reason He set us free was so we could come to Him freely. He doesn't force you but extends His hand and welcomes you."

Then, expressing that freedom, I wiggled and shook in a way that made the chains around me begin to loosen. At that moment, I was reliving for them the night when my own chains fell off.

The chains slammed to the floor. Echoes from the impact filled that theater. Then the sound of weeping swelled up.

I shouted again, "If you have never accepted Jesus into your heart, and today you want Him to break your chains, stand with me and join me in the front."

I knew that the Lord was touching their hearts and healing many of them because I could see how their eyes and their bodies moved with new lightness and energy. I believe that the sound of their feet pounding down the black theater stairs thundered through the kingdom of darkness, as these souls were getting ready to step into the light.

In a few moments hundreds of kids stood with their heads bowed and their hearts opened as they accepted Jesus into their lives. Many who woke up that day thinking it would be a normal day at school got something different.

They met Jesus.

As we prayed together, He set them free from the chains that bound them, and in a way He set me free as well. I had learned that God was moving and nothing would stop it.

Feeling the weight of those chains that day, chains that bind the hearts of most of the kids in high school, was something I had not expected. If I had not obeyed God would any of these students have ever heard the message of salvation? Would they ever have been reached?

From the time Jesus had called me, I had longed for high school kids to know Him, and I had done my best to obey. But now I was compelled. The picture of Jesus breaking chains off kids bound in darkness made my calling in life clear.

So many times students are left chained simply because those who are called to help them get free never say yes. I am sure God could have sent someone else to reach that campus at some later time, but what if the opportunity this day had been lost? Could it be that the answer for the youth of America lies in our ability to grab hold of God, knowing that when we reach out to model His love, He shows up? What if it's not enough anymore for people or churches or ministries to measure success by the number in attendance? What if we measure our success by knowing God and making Him known?

I still did not know the extent of how God would use me to bring revival to the high schools of America, but He wanted me to go and step out, and now, more than ever, I was ready.

6

JESUS LOVES GANGBANGERS

NOT LONG AFTER GOD BROKE OUT IN those two schools, Elk Grove High and Laguna Creek High, I started getting invitations to preach in various Bible clubs in other schools. Our city wasn't that big, and word travels fast when hundreds are getting saved.

By December 2010, I was preaching on six high school campuses, seeing Jesus fill gyms and theaters in all the schools I went to. I didn't change anything I was doing because I knew it was working: Students were coming to Christ. I would often take moments to sit and look back on all that was taking place, pondering how a former atheist, so broken only a few years before, got to this place of seeing the power of God save so many.

With Jesus Club meetings now running three hundred, four hundred, five hundred students on different campuses, I was in awe and full of faith about what God was capable of doing. Every chance I got with friends, family or people I met, I would share the stories of God moving in these schools—although most people I told didn't have the same passion I had since they had not seen what I had seen.

And I know, it sounds crazy, right? It was crazy. All I can say is the Jesus Clubs increased by the hundreds and donations to support the ministry to them began to come in. I had learned to do so much with so little that any financial support we received truly was a bonus.

The doubt I once had wondering "If God could do it" had now turned into "When was God going to do it?" And my answer was ever so clear: "*Now* and with *everyone!*" I didn't need to pray anymore to see if God wanted to save the schools of my city; I just needed to wait and see which campus would open first.

About a year and a half had passed since I had first preached in a high school. Now more than two thousand students had made a profession of faith to follow Jesus. Many other Christians in the area wanted God to move in their high schools, too. And their eager hearts were drawing revival to their fellow classmates.

One school I was invited to was probably one of my most memorable to this day. I remember the campus for its reputation, which changed in the years I was there.

I had been approached by a student at Valley High named John who was one of the leaders of the club there and who also had connection with Lisa, the Jesus Club president at Laguna. It was a campus in a rough neighborhood where students fell prey to their surroundings. Gangs and drugs plagued this school—but where darkness was, the light was about to shine brighter.

The teachers and the staff I met there were some of the most amazing people on the planet. And so were the students, but their surroundings made it hard for them to see the light. They were so caught up in drugs and gangs, their only hope seemed to be in the temporary pleasures they felt.

After seeing so many open hearts at Laguna, I couldn't wait to get to this school. *How hard could it be?* I thought. I mean, it was only five or six miles from Laguna.

I remember meeting John to scope out the school. I had learned early on to know my mission field. I could see in the eyes of the kids we passed the longing to belong and be part of a family.

"Take me to every gang leader," I said to John. "I want to meet them and let them know that if they need anything, to come talk to me."

One after the other, I went around with him meeting the Bloods and the Crips, the Nortenos and Surenos. They greeted John, but showed some reservation toward this guy with him—me. John introduced me and told them I was his good friend. It was evident that I needed to speak for myself with these tatted-up gangbangers who didn't have to listen to a word I said.

At first they were standoffish, but after a few weeks of my coming and showing them love, those hardened hearts began to welcome me into their crews even when John wasn't present.

"Brian!" they would shout from the other side of the quad as I was walking by during their lunchtime. I would run over, shaking their hands at first, but before long giving them hugs. I could see the greatness inside them and knew they had never seen it in themselves. One of the students I will never forget was this kid who had health issues due to a gunshot wound in his neck.

Slowly but surely they started to trust that I wasn't just someone telling them what they should do; I was someone who was showing them how to walk out change.

"We have to hold a meeting," I said to John after about a month. "And soon. I have met enough people that I think they will come."

Thursdays were the days I had free, as I was on other campuses the other days. After talking out the details, we set it up to have our first Jesus Club meeting the following week. Now, I had been at Elk Grove, a primarily white school, and Laguna, a rough school, but neither compared to Valley High.

How will meetings work here, if and when all these gangs get saved? I wondered.

The following Thursday came and, as usual, I arrived a little early, signed in and headed to the classroom where we were going to meet. I wish I could recall the room number we met in in those early days at Valley High School, but I cannot. What I do remember was that our first meeting was anything but spectacular.

As the bell rang, I sat in the front of the classroom facing the quad, waiting eagerly to see who would show up. When fifteen minutes had passed, and about five new students had come in, I knew I had better start talking or they would probably get bored and leave. I realized that these kids were not Laguna or Elk Grove students. It was going to take more than a few hellos at lunch to get them to a meeting.

I stood and started speaking and preaching the Gospel as I had done many other times, but this was different. This room felt heavy and disconnected from God. Fairly certain that no one was listening, I nonetheless said, "If you want to encounter this love I was speaking of, I want you to stand to your feet."

Now in a room of hundreds, if certain people don't respond you don't really notice. But in a room of five, it's really noticeable.

As I paused a few seconds, the five students stood up. Joy filled my heart instantly, and I knew that God was going to invade this campus. I felt as though I was back at square one, but there was hope.

After the meeting I walked with John to his class and we began to dream for Valley High. We decided that the best way to get students to come would be to bring in boxes of pizza (I had told him that I had done this for Laguna) and walk around campus at lunchtime, showing that we had free food.

"They may not want the Bible," I said with a laugh, "but they sure will want free pizza!"

The club leaders and I wanted to move the meeting into a bigger space, so we got permission for the wrestling room. It too wasn't far from where every student hung out during lunch, and we could fit in 250, if we set up chairs.

When the next Thursday rolled around, everything was in place. Now this was not my first time getting ready in a room like this or preparing a message, believing that God would save hundreds, but that didn't take away the feeling of nervousness. I was never nervous of something going wrong in the meetings; I just wanted God to show up, because if He did, I knew lives would change.

The chairs were set up, the pizza was bought, and, although I didn't have a mic because there was no sound system I could use, I did have a loud voice. All we needed now was the students.

When the lunch bell rang, John and I and a few other leaders from the Jesus Club took a couple of boxes of pizza and started to walk the campus quad. It wasn't long before kids called out, "Hey, can we get some?"

"Yes," we shouted back. "Meet us in the wrestling room."

More and more students began to ask if they, too, could have some pizza, and we responded the same way: "Meet us in the wrestling room."

We headed back with around 25 minutes to preach. When we walked into the wrestling room, every one of the 250 seats was filled—and this was only first lunch. Like Laguna, Valley High had two lunches.

I couldn't believe it. It worked.

I mean, they were there for pizza, but, *Hey,* I thought, *who knows what Jesus can do in 25 minutes?*

I began to preach. I looked at those gang members, who just a month prior were complete strangers to me. Now they were hearing about Jesus. Bloods and Crips and Nortenos and Surenos all sitting together. The next lunch was the same and, from the classroom to the wrestling room, five hundred students responded to the call to accept Jesus.

What amazed me was not that their hands went up or even that they spoke the words to accept Jesus into their hearts. What amazed me was the fruit of repentance that followed. Several of the students who continued coming began to tell me how gang life wasn't for them anymore. They had had a heart change, and it was now leading to a life change.

"Why do you fight for a color you don't even own?" I shouted one Thursday at the Jesus Club. "Are you Crayola? Why do you fight for streets when most of your families can barely afford their rent? Why do you die for streets that you will never own?"

I was filled with so much love that day I couldn't bear any longer the thought of these gang members, who had been attending our Valley High meetings for a few weeks now, leaving the same way they had come in. The fact that they were attending Jesus Club meetings wasn't good enough for me. They had to have a changed life—and just a few changing wasn't enough. I wanted them all to change. Call me harsh; I'll call it love—because that's what I felt when I spoke this truth to those many gangbangers in the wrestling room that day.

I had won much favor with their leaders early on. Maybe it was the simple fact that I took the time every week to ask how they were—and also feed them pizza. Many times my quick stops to say hello turned into deep conversations. And what started with a few gang members coming in as spectators turned into whole neighborhoods of gangs listening to the Good News.

So I stood there shouting, as I did at every Thursday meeting, about what Jesus did and the price He paid. But this day something was different. Every week there were always a few kids who tried to act cool by talking or telling jokes, but on this day no one was saying anything.

I had been talking about the blood that Jesus shed to cover their sins. Maybe the blood was something they could relate to. As my time was running out and the bell was about to ring, I did what I did every week. I led it back to receiving Jesus.

I was about to ask "if anyone in the room wants to receive Jesus" when I was interrupted. With no warning, one of the gang members sitting about halfway back stood to his feet. All eyes turned from me to him to see what he was going to do. I stopped speaking, wondering the same thing. Sweat began to drip down my neck as I stood there waiting.

That's when something miraculous happened.

With boldness in his voice he shouted, "What must I do to be saved?"

At first I didn't believe what my ears were hearing. This sounded like the Bible days. Maybe the words he was speaking came from a message I had preached a few weeks earlier or from someone in his life telling this guy that he needed to be saved. You know, the Bible says that some plant, some water, but Christ makes it grow. I don't know if I was the planter or the waterer, but Jesus was making this seed grow—and fast.

I was shocked—so shocked that I didn't realize I hadn't given him an answer.

"What must you do to be saved?" I finally said in more of a stutter than a voice.

Then I gathered myself. "You repent and give up this gang life. You trade in your old life for an amazing new one. This repentance is joyful," I said.

With tears in his eyes, he said, "Okay."

And he slid past the other gang members sitting in his row and walked up to the front.

Just as bold as he was in his 'hood, so he was in that wrestling room. With every eye watching, he received Jesus.

I can't give you an exact number of how many students in gangs gave up their rags and colors and street life, but it was enough for the principal to pull me into his office one afternoon after Jesus Club and encourage me to keep doing what I was doing, because it was working.

Gangs were dropping out.

Valley High was now in full-blown revival.

With hundreds attending the Valley High Jesus Club and so much change taking place on the campus, I thought it was time for another Jesus Rally. The student club leaders and administration agreed it was a good idea. The only thing the staff required was that we hire police officers to be on duty, because bringing so many gangs together after school could cause problems. They gave me the rundown of what it would take to make this day happen and finally all was set.

Word began to spread throughout the school that a Jesus Rally was going to happen. The hundreds gathering weekly invited their friends. Free food was a major draw as well, especially on a campus that doesn't get much free anything.

After months of planning, the day finally came. The Jesus Club team and I arrived early for setup in the gym, getting the stage, sound and food all ready. In just a few hours the doors would open and the moment of truth would come.

Would this gang-infested school respond as a whole to the Jesus Rally? The talk among the students seemed good; they were excited. And so were we.

I have to admit that my excitement took a hit when one of our team members overheard the police officers talking.

"No one is going to come to this Jesus thing," one officer said. "It's after school and it's about Jesus."

When I heard the expectations of the cops, I bowed my head and felt all the more confidence that God was going to do what the police units themselves could not do: bring peace among the gangs.

I prayed this prayer quietly. "Jesus, You have heard them. Prove them wrong." I was interrupted by the sound of someone calling my name.

I looked up and saw one of the students I knew standing in the back doorway. I walked over to him.

"What's the matter, Andrei?" I asked him.

"They won't let me in the rally because of how much trouble I've been in."

"Who won't let you in?"

"The staff."

I noticed then that the students were being screened before being let through the doors. I knew Andrei's history—he was a drug dealer and most of the people in his life had lost hope in him. I had asked him many times to come to our Jesus Club meetings during lunch and was always given the same answer: "Maybe next week."

I was hesitant to let him in, not wanting to disobey school authority. But in the end I decided it was better to deal with the staff for letting him in than deal with God for keeping him out.

"Come in," I said quietly. "Sit down and don't say anything."

I knew that this might be Andrei's only chance to hear the Good News, and I couldn't pass it up.

Not all of the kids who showed up at the door were able to get in; those who did take seats numbered close to eight hundred. I picked up the mic, welcomed everyone and so it began. From rappers to free T-shirts, the Gospel was displayed in everything we did, and walls in many hearts began coming down.

The students seemed to be children again in that atmosphere—not worried about their appearance or what street they were from. And for some this was the first time ever experiencing that feeling.

Finally it was time for the Gospel. A good friend of mine named Darwin Benjamin, *aka* Rev. D., got up and started speaking about his own life in the streets. He talked about the drugs and the money and the emptiness it left him—and even the cost of his own child's life.

Filled with emotion and passion and love, he poured out every ounce of his heart, trusting that God would deposit it in the right place.

I looked around that gym full of kids and wondered what the policeman who had said no one would show up must be thinking. I wondered what the staff who feared that a riot might break out must be thinking.

At that moment you could have heard a pin drop. Then Rev. D. said something that in a few minutes would shake the lives of everyone in that gym, including me.

"Bring me garbage cans," he said.

Confused, we rushed to find some.

"Put them in the front," he said.

So we did. My mind was thinking a million thoughts. What did these garbage cans have to do with the Gospel?

"If you are in this room today," Rev. D. said to the quiet students, "and you have never accepted Jesus into your heart and you want to, if you want to have Him and only Him, I want you to stand up."

The scuffling of shoes on bleachers and the gym floor was the immediate response.

"If you want to receive Jesus, I want you to do something first," he continued. "These garbage cans are here because I want you to trash the things trashing you. The Gospel isn't for no chumps. It's for those who will be real. If you want to be saved, bring your condoms, your weapons and drugs and anything else that would hinder you from God."

Within seconds all but about fifty of those eight hundred students ran to the front and started to empty their pockets and backpacks into the garbage cans. One of the students was the young gangbanger who had been crippled by a gunshot wound. Many others that I passed by in the halls every week on my way to preach came with tears in their eyes. My heart was joyful because whether they came to know Jesus through my message or not, they were meeting Him, and that's all that mattered.

And that's when I saw him. Andrei, the kid that was almost stopped from entering, standing in the front with his hands lifted to accept Jesus. His "Maybe next week" turned into a salvation encounter at a Jesus Rally in his gym.

This was the Gospel. This was what it meant to go after the lost sheep. You never know when that "Maybe next week" will turn into the yes that will change a life.

I wish I could have captured the emotions of that day. The Bible says that signs and wonders follow those who believe. And what happened was a sign and a wonder. Jesus' name was lifted up, and He drew all to Him.

Valley High was never the same after that. Think about it. Most students have memories of their schools filled with everything *but* God. But for those in that school that year, their high school memories will have everything to do *with* God.

7

ENCOUNTER WITH A GOD WHO HEALS

ANOTHER CAMPUS NOT TOO FAR FROM what was taking place in Elk Grove was seeing a move of God, as their Jesus Club moved from a classroom to the gym in a few weeks. I had been invited to speak at Mesa Verde High School. And that invitation quickly turned into my coming every week. The Jesus Club was led by another teen from my church at that time. We wanted to see Jesus do there what He was doing in other schools.

We were amazed when He did even more.

For the longest time, to be honest, I had wanted to see God break out in crazy miracles. Some of the books I had read the past summer about revivals talked about the miracles that ran alongside them. Those stories gave me faith. I never want to chase miracles, but it was evident that when Jesus shows up, healing in every way has to take place—healing of the heart, the mind, the soul and the body.

Still, never once did I think God would have me be part of something like what I was reading, until one lunchtime Jesus Club changed everything.

As the gym was filling with students, I was being filled with faith. I had just read in Scripture about Jesus healing all those who came in contact with Him, so I called for anyone who wanted to see God's power demonstrated in a miracle to come forward. I knew there were many skeptics in the room. Not that they had ever voiced it, but by the expressions people made I knew some hadn't truly surrendered their hearts to Jesus.

This school wasn't gang infested like Valley High, and the students didn't struggle with poverty, but the heart issues they faced were the same. A heart is a heart whether you have money or nothing. And Jesus didn't treat anyone any differently—from the rich young ruler to the poor sick ones, everyone needed Him and He loved them all.

So I shouted out to the hundreds of kids in the gym, "Who's sick in this room or has a problem or pain in your body?"

I didn't know where else to start but to ask straight up if they needed God to heal them. While the seconds passed I kept recalling page after page I had read of miracles in the Bible and in the various revival books.

Out of the crowd a girl stood up and, in front of everyone, said that she had been partially deaf her whole life.

"Can Jesus heal my hearing?" she asked.

My heart dropped to the ground with excitement and with nervousness. Jesus had to come through. I mean, this was black and white. Either she would hear or she wouldn't. And I was definitely banking on the first one.

"Jesus can heal you," I said, but my voice was a little shaky.

I called down some of the students from the bleachers to stand with me and asked everyone else to pray as well. Those of us standing there surrounded her, and I placed my hands on both sides of her head, just hovering over her ears without touching her.

I knew that every eye was glued to this scene at the front of the gym, as if spellbound. Everyone wanted to see if Jesus could really heal. And truth be told, so did I.

I began to pray. "Jesus," I said, "You're not a liar. If You healed the deaf in the Bible You can do it again. Be healed in Jesus' name."

With everyone silent and waiting to see what would happen next, I looked at her and began to ask if she could notice any difference. In about ten seconds she began to scream and cry.

"I can hear you! I can hear you!" she shouted.

My first thought was, *Jesus, You're so real.*

It's not that I doubted He could heal this girl, but seeing her set free in that gym from her deafness filled my heart with faith. Many started rejoicing, jumping up and down and shouting.

I heard later that some of the kids didn't believe this was real, but it didn't matter. All that mattered was the girl walked in not hearing and now she could hear. The story spread quickly through the school, and students began coming to the Jesus Club to see what God could do.

Shortly after this, another miracle took place in the biggest school in Elk Grove, Franklin High School. I had driven past that school many times. My dream was that one day I'd be able to share the Gospel there and see students saved. About three thousand students attended the school at that time, and the Scripture about Peter preaching at Pentecost, where three thousand were saved, often came to my mind.

After seeing God move in other schools in Elk Grove, I got a message from a student at Franklin. She told me how the students on the campus needed Jesus. She invited me to come as a guest speaker to the Bible club there, the title I often held when going to a new school.

As we talked, she mentioned that Club Rush Day was coming, when all the clubs would be setting up in the quad to show the students what they had to offer.

"Perfect," I said. "I'll be there."

On Club Rush Day, I walked through the office of this more modern campus to get my pass. Then I headed for the door that I guessed led to the quad and pushed it open, hoping I had the right one.

As I walked outside into the bright sunlight, I was startled to see so many students setting up. There was the Band Club, the Chess Club, the Comic Book Club, the Latino Club and many more that I couldn't even imagine would be clubs.

"Brian!"

It was the student member of the Jesus Club calling me. "This is our table, the table for the Jesus Club."

Now, I hadn't come like all the others with food and props and candy, but I had an idea.

"Do you have something we can write on?" I asked.

She rummaged around and found some construction paper.

"Okay," I said. "Write *Free Prayer and Free Healing.*"

All the other clubs offered sweets and other food, but I sensed that God was going to do something in the hearts of these students that would fill them for more than five minutes.

We got to work writing *Free Prayer and Free Healing* on the pieces of construction paper and propped them on the table. As the bell signaled the beginning of lunch, I looked around at the number of students signing up for other clubs but few came our way. I could tell the kids were a little discouraged. The students weren't going to come to us, so we were going to have to go to them.

I motioned to a few of the Jesus Club guys to follow me, and we walked up to three punk rockers standing nearby. One of them had a sling on his arm. *This is perfect,* I said to myself.

I asked what they thought of Jesus, just to start small talk and knowing I was going to get a negative answer. They laughed and said they didn't believe in God because He wasn't real. These were perfect candidates to be future members of the Jesus Club.

I looked at the guys with me and then to the rockers, and said to the one wearing a sling, "What's wrong with your arm, man?"

"I sprained it and it hurts really bad. I can't move it," he said.

I knew this was the time to show them Jesus was very real and that He really wanted to encounter them.

So I said, "How about I make you a deal? I will pray with the help of your friends to a God you don't believe in and say is not real. If He heals your arm, He exists, and if He doesn't, He doesn't exist."

They looked at each other, smiling as if they knew for sure they had this bet won.

"Deal?" I asked.

"Okay."

I told the guy's two friends to put their hands on his shoulder and to repeat a prayer after me. I was banking on the verse where Jesus said if two or three come together in His name, then He is there with them. The verse doesn't say two or three believers or pastors. It just says two or three, and we had that. These kids weren't all cleaned up and churched. They had skinny jeans and wild hairstyles, but to my amazement they put their hands on their friend's shoulder, willing to see what God would do.

With faith in my heart, and knowing there was no turning back, I said, "Now repeat this after me: 'Jesus, we command healing on this sprained shoulder. No more pain, in Jesus' name.'"

No sparks flew when these atheist boys prayed to Jesus for the first time, but something shifted. I know that some people think a connection with Jesus is mostly about appearances. By that, I mean instead of teaching people how to be disciples, they are taught how to look like good American churchgoers.

This prayer for healing by three punk rockers was not about trying to change their appearance. These guys had a chance to hear and see Jesus move, and that would be enough to change their lives.

I told the young man to move his arm. As he began to move it, the craziest, most shocked look on his face said it all. His friends looked shocked as well, as their buddy could now move his arm freely.

"I can't believe it," he said. "There's no pain. That's impossible."

"Take off your sling and do something you couldn't do before," I said.

They had looks on their faces of total disbelief, but they couldn't explain away this miracle that had happened for their own friend.

God had come; there was no doubt about it. With amazement and many curse words, they said how they couldn't believe it. How a God they were denying only a few seconds earlier had touched their friend's arm.

I asked them if they wanted to receive Jesus into their hearts—not just pray in His name but start a relationship with Him.

With smiles they all replied, "Yes!"

In the quad, with much going on around us, we all bowed our heads, and they asked the Lord into their hearts.

About a week after Club Rush Day, we held our first Jesus Club meeting at Franklin, with me as guest speaker. Not knowing how many to expect, the club members had reserved the theater, which held three hundred. Theaters, auditoriums and gyms became the normal meeting spots. After all, we knew that classrooms would be too small.

But as we opened the doors that day only three people came, one of whom was a Muslim. The kids I had met at the Club Rush Day didn't even show up.

Great! I thought. *Here we go again back to the small meetings!*

But, regardless, I was happy to be at this school. I still preached as though the place was packed, wondering if this message of Jesus was penetrating their hearts.

Through that next week I pondered what might change this small number. How would we see this theater filled?

In just a few weeks, through word of mouth, three hundred students filled that theater in Franklin High. And when the call of salvation was given, hands were raised, tears were wept and many came to know Jesus. And this was but the start of an entire school year of revival.

When I thought about it, it amazed me that for decades people have believed the lie that Jesus is not wanted in schools. I have discovered something very different. True, students do not want religion, but they desperately desire a relationship with their Creator.

In the 1960s in America I believe the devil overplayed his hand. Atheistic views to remove prayer from schools, and the religious stigma associated with it, dominated, and the results of those years were soon evident in hearts of rebellion in many high schools. Our modern generations do not even know basic biblical truths.

But I could see that changing.

A few years after miracles at Mesa Verde and Franklin, I would hear Lou Engle say: "Where there are riots, under the ground rumbles revival." Even though the door to prayer and Bible reading in public schools was closed corporately, another door to a massive revival was swinging wide open more than fifty years later.

I am one of many witnesses to the fact that public school grounds are becoming tents of revival. These students at Mesa Verde and Franklin and the other high schools were not mocking God; they simply had never heard about Him. And when given the opportunity, they were eager to meet Him.

With all boldness I can say that America is ready for a harvest—more than ever before. This nation is like a tree with fruit that's fully ripe and about to fall off the branches. And if not caught, it will go to waste and rot away. This is the picture of our youth. We have a window of time in which their hearts are receptive to the Gospel.

In going to school after school I always leave amazed. That day when Jesus healed the girl who was deaf, I got into my vehicle and could not drive very far before I began weeping, because none of this was fabricated by me. I was not yet twenty years old. I wasn't a great preacher. I didn't have a Bible degree. And I had never even had a heart for high schools before going to that camp.

But I did have a yielded heart. I was able to partner with the God of miracles every lunchtime and see Him move in many lives.

I realized one other thing as I pondered this over the coming weeks. It was no method or strategy that was saving these campuses; it was a sovereign move of God.

It was a loving Father answering the cry of a desperate kid who had no idea what he was doing, but was asking Him to save the high schools.

I spent many nights and mornings with the Lord. In those times I would cry out, "God, I pray that I would know You. But I also pray that You would know me."

I wanted to stay obedient. Because I knew that would change history.

8

PRAYER WOULD BE RESTORED

IT WAS WINTER BREAK, DECEMBER 2010. Many amazing things had happened since God spoke the crazy word that He was going to save America's high schools. And from that, prayer would be restored. Up until this time the Jesus Clubs had experienced the salvation part of that promise—a couple thousand kids had come to Jesus. But where did the whole restoring prayer piece fit in?

The worship band I played bass for asked me to go with them to a prayer meeting that Monday night of winter break. They told me that some high school students had started a sixty-hour prayer meeting, and, to be honest, I didn't believe it. What would students pray about for sixty hours? And why?

I had to go and see what was going on. As we made the hour or so drive south from Elk Grove to Manteca, a sense of mystery lingered in my heart. We pulled into the driveway of a church building and I thought, *Wow! This is huge. It must be a pretty large prayer meeting.* The church looked as if it would hold at least a thousand people.

But we kept going around to the back and stopped in front of a small building off to the side, more like a portable room, with lights on.

"Here we are," someone said.

I'm not going to lie. I was not excited to see another tiny prayer meeting. I know that sounds bad—and it was. But it's what I thought. Usually in really small meetings I had not found that I felt God like crazy.

We unloaded our gear and walked into the room. The young man leading the meeting greeted us. He nodded toward the nearly thirty teenagers there, telling us they were students at various local high schools and youth groups who wanted to pray for revival to come. They had heard about what God was doing in Elk Grove and, along with others, had been praying and crying out to God for their schools to be saved.

I looked at some students praying on their faces, others pacing back and forth, all asking the Lord to save their friends. There was nothing glamorous about the prayer meeting. There were no fancy lights or a famous worship team or pizza or games. There was only hunger in this room. So much hunger that it fueled these students to pray for hours upon hours.

I was amazed. I had thought I was just about the only one who had a burning vision for high schools. At that moment I was a lot like Elijah, who thought he alone was left of the true worshipers of God, only to discover there were seven thousand others who had not bowed their knees to Baal.

I was in awe and really humbled. Our team set up in the already worshipful atmosphere and began to play. The desperation in the room only grew as the students took turns with the mic, praying for revival to come.

They called out the names of high schools and high school districts one by one. I glanced around and saw that they had printed the names of schools onto sheets of paper and taped the sheets to the wall. My eyes scanned the pages with names I had never heard of until I saw one that made my heart leap.

Elk Grove Unified.

Part of me jumped with thankfulness and another part of me felt the weight of a prayer burden for my city. These praying kids were showing me the key to having revival break out. Matthew 9 came alive to me. That Scripture talks about the way Jesus saw broken people, prayed that the Lord of the harvest would send out laborers, and then anointed His men to become the answer to their own prayers.

As our worship ministry came to a close that evening, a young man, maybe a little older than I was, approached me and said that God had given him a word for me.

"My name is Sammy," he said. "I am a part of the Circuit Riders."

I knew very little of this ministry at that time, only that they were doing things for God in America. I never would have thought that in the years to come the whole Circuit Rider community would be some of my best friends.

"Hi, I'm Brian. What did God tell you?" I asked.

Taking a moment to think before he spoke, he finally said, "The Lord told me there is still a sound in you that has not been released or heard in America. And this sound will set many free. That's all God told me," he said.

I was amazed once more. Here was this young guy who didn't know me, and as he spoke his words settled in my spirit. I wondered if the sound I carried was salvation? Would it possibly set high schools all over America free?

I thanked him joyfully with a handshake, which led to a hug.

As we drove off that night, the sight and sound of those fervent students played over and over in my mind. Those kids who didn't have a fancy room to pray in or the best equipment to use had wrecked my life.

Once back home I found myself praying differently. As I lay there in bed, my heart was grieved in a good way. I had truly fallen in love with my city. And when I thought about the condition it was in, I could no longer just preach. I had to pray.

The next day I woke up early and said this: "God, I will not leave in the morning to preach any more at any school unless I feel Your presence."

I made a vow in my heart with God that I would wake up at five a.m. to seek Him and would preach only if it came from a place of hunger for seeing souls saved. My life was now marked by those three hours I had spent at that youth room in Manteca, California.

It was a turning point. Going forward from that time I wanted everything related to the Jesus Clubs to be fueled by prayer and intercession. I knew that prayer is the greatest place to get a burden for the lost—but we are not meant to stay there holding that burden and ignoring the great Commandment of Jesus to go and make disciples.

I spent the rest of that week driving up to Manteca to pray with the kids, and my hunger for God began to grow.

I don't remember how I got my hands on the book called *Why Revival Tarries* by Leonard Ravenhill, but I do remember it was like wood to this already kindled fire in my heart. It became more and more evident that my calling to pray wasn't just emotion, but unction.

During that whole Christmas break I sought God like crazy. I prayed incessantly. I prayed in the Spirit. My heart was so set on schools being touched by God that I went all out in prayer and intercession. During the day words and cries of mercy flowed from my lips. At night tears flowed for the schools to be saved in the Elk Grove Unified School District.

My heart was no longer satisfied for the numbers I was seeing come to Christ. I had to see more and more of Jesus changing lives.

God must have noticed the change. There were nights when I was in bed ready to fall asleep, and He would tell me to get up and drive to one of the schools in the district.

I would say, "God, it's ten o'clock at night. I'm tired and have to preach tomorrow."

He again would speak to my heart. I can't say I was never grumpy about it, but I would get up, get dressed, climb into my car and go.

One December night when the Lord told me to go pray, I could hear the winter-season rain hitting my bedroom windows.

I thought, *Lord, You have to be kidding me. I can pray from my bed and not get wet by the rain, right?*
But I felt Him urging me to go to Elk Grove High.

Some minutes later, I was sitting in my car, cold and tired, in the front parking lot facing Elk Grove Boulevard. *I must be crazy,* I thought. *Here I am. It's pouring rain, and I'm going to go pray by myself in front of the school. Well, I drove this far. . . .*
My hand reached for the door handle. There was no point in even trying to keep dry since I was about to get soaked. I walked to the front of the dark school and looked at the elk that I passed by on my way to preach. Then I stopped and knelt before it, and that's when it hit me.

I began to weep and weep feeling the heart of God for the pain in this school. I guess my simply getting out of bed and leaving the house and driving my car and getting soaked brought about God's willingness to trust me with something sacred: His heart.

As I began to cry out to the Lord to save this campus and every campus in the city, I forgot about the rain and the cold. All that was on my mind and heart was students knowing Jesus.

"Hello?" A voice shouted at me and bright lights flooded me. "What are you doing here after school hours?"

I tried to focus past the blinding lights. I realized it was the Elk Grove police. A little scared and shaken from being interrupted while praying, I shouted, "I'm praying. I'm praying for this campus."

I think the officers were not sure what to do with that. After a few moments one of them said, "Well, um, have a great night. And be safe."

They climbed quickly back into their patrol car, glad, I feel sure, to avoid getting any wetter.

As they drove off, my heart once again broke for the school. I had many nights like this—minus the cops. That happened only once. This season for me was truly amazing as I witnessed what God was doing.

My family at times asked me if I thought of anything else but campuses, but the dream God had placed in my heart was more than a daytime hobby; it was becoming a mission that had to be fulfilled. It even was more than a ministry. It was the thing I would give my life to. And the question of how God would restore prayer in the Elk Grove schools moved to the forefront of my heart.

The winter break was ending. School was coming back into session. As the new year of 2011 was about to start, I asked the leaders of the Elk Grove Jesus Clubs to meet with me.

As a few leaders from different schools and I sat together at our favorite meeting spot—a pizza place right off the freeway—I told them that my heart had encountered something it had never encountered before. I began to tell them how God was gripping me in the place of prayer.

I declared, "It's no longer enough to preach. We must pray."

As we talked I realized that what He had spoken to me at Spirit West Coast was making a lot more sense. We all agreed to listen for God's guidance about this and see how we could do this corporately, not just individually.

One day I was with some of the student leaders and said, "What if we had prayer meetings on campus? We would pray and cry out to God. No one would preach; we would only pray."

They said they loved the idea. They, too, wanted to see a greater manifestation of God.

We decided to call it "City Fire." Our desire was to bring students from all over the city together at one place to pray and ask God for two specific things: for the salvation of our friends and family, and for an awakening to come across the high schools in America. We wanted to rebuild the altar of prayer, believing that revival fire would come the way it had in Elijah's days. If the altar was rebuilt, we believed the fire would fall.

We grew more and more excited about this vision of prayer. We contacted youth groups from a number of churches and asked them to come and pray with us. Then we got permission to hold the prayer meeting in the little theater at Laguna Creek High after school hours on a Friday night in mid-January.

I was comfortable in the little theater—a room I knew very well from preaching there every week. I had many memories of God showing up. I could still see the faces and tears of students who had encountered Jesus. I could still hear the messages I had preached and remember how God had broken in.

As we finished setting up the small sound system the night of the first City Fire, everything was ready. Fifteen teenagers who were regular attendees of our Jesus Clubs, along with those of us who planned the event, attended the gathering.

Not having anyone to lead worship, we joyfully plugged our iPods into the school sound system. Scrolling through all of our options, we settled on music by Jesus Culture—a group from Bethel Church in Redding, California. Our presentation wasn't fancy, but we did feel the presence of God.

Everyone came with good intentions, but there was a problem. No one knew what to do next. And truth be told I wasn't 100 percent sure how to lead them. Though this may sound funny, no one knew how to pray.

As the kids were looking around at each other, wondering what to do at a prayer meeting, it hit me that this was all too common for those of us in our generation. There are gatherings to help kids draw closer to God and to play ice breaker games and to sit and hear a message, but I realized that few of us have ever been taught to pray—especially together in a setting like this.

The Scripture in Luke 11 of the disciples asking Jesus to teach them to pray made much more sense to me that night. I always liked it that out of everything Jesus' followers could have asked Him to teach them, they said, "Teach us to pray!"

For my part, I stood there, silent, because I was not sure how all this was going to play out. All I knew was God said gather and pray—and His original word to me that prayer would be restored in high schools kept echoing in my heart. One more thought came to me:

The prayer meeting about a month before had shaken my life, and I wanted the people in the room to experience the same.

Suddenly, the Lord said to me, *If they don't pray, you pray.*

But what did that mean?

Wanting to be obedient, I started to walk back and forth, speaking out loud the desire I felt inside for God to visit our city. I asked God with all of my heart that night to save the campus we were on and save our generation. It wasn't my words that motivated anyone; I believe it was my desperation. If God wasn't going to show up, then this was all for nothing. But if our desperate hearts would provoke Him to save our city, we had a chance.

Soon afterward, the students started to do the same, asking God to save their families and friends and to fill the schools with His presence. It was as though we began to hunger and thirst for God. There was no hype, just the desire to know Him. A sense of freedom seemed to break out in our praying. I felt that they were beginning to understand Jesus' heart for the lost.

We held several City Fire prayer meetings on Friday nights over the next few months. Attendance grew steadily; anywhere from 25 to 50 students came. Sometimes local pastors joined us. But most important, our intimacy with God was growing.

There was no preaching as I mentioned. Just prayer. We would hand someone the mic and say, "Pray." And one by one the kids would pour out their hearts for their schools.

"Save the high schools of Elk Grove!" they would say. "Save the high schools of America!"

Here's the amazing thing: You could feel the tangible presence of God. I had never experienced anything like it. And the number of physical healings that took place was incredible. Many students witnessed the healings and began praying for the sick themselves. We were learning more about what happens when you cultivate the presence of God. Sickness cannot dwell where God is.

One night one of the girls brought along a friend who did not believe in Jesus. As we were praying I handed the mic to this unsaved girl. She took it and said, "God, I don't know if You are real, but if You are, touch my life."

That young girl started to weep there on the spot. And God met her cry.

On Friday nights when the various Laguna Creek High School teams had home games, the cheerleaders and athletes who attended the Jesus Club would run into the little theater during halftime, where we would pray for them, and then they would run back to the game. It truly was a place where God dwelled.

We built a pillar of prayer in that city for what God was going to do in America. And in a small way, the Supreme Court case of 1962 that found a 22-word voluntary school prayer to be unconstitutional was being countered. Students weren't reciting a short prayer, however. They were gathering to seek God and cry out to Him with all their hearts. And they were also praying quietly in their schools during the day. They would do things like pray at people's lockers when the owners of those lockers weren't there, asking God to save those kids.

City Fire met until the end of the school year, six months of prayer for revival and awakening—and another Jesus movement.

It was during this time that God started to form the DNA of One Voice Student Missions—the desire of my heart to bring prayer and missions together in high schools. It was being shaped with a double outreach: students being saved as the Gospel was preached and prayer being established in the high schools.

One afternoon I sat down with several students to talk about what we sensed God wanted to do next. I had been watching videos of a ministry known as TheCall, led by Lou Engle. I had stumbled on his videos and was inspired by the massive prayer gatherings of young people. As we talked about the impact of that ministry, we dreamed of having something like that in our city, but specifically for high school students.

So what started as a small group in a theater led to a gathering that August with more than a thousand high school students. I called it the One Voice Prayer Gathering. It was held in a barn in Elk Grove owned by a man named Big Al. Many of us stood there in the hot sun for twelve hours with amazing worship team leaders such as Catherine Mullins and Melissa How and many more. Principals, teachers, students and people from a number of churches came from all over the city to join together, believing that campus missionaries would arise in America.

It wasn't long after that, beginning the following January 2012, that I began to travel and organize One Voice Prayer Gatherings all over California—from Redding, in the northern part of the state, down to Los Angeles. I asked God to save the high schools of America, and invited churches and cities to do the same.

I won't go into great detail of these gatherings, but I truly know that today we are still reaping the fruit from those times of prayer in which students were mobilized in cities all over the state to come pray. Some of the events were held in the Cascade Theatre in Redding; the Memorial Auditorium in Sacramento; Cal State East Bay College in Hayward; and the Dome in Bakersfield.

As the end of the school year was approaching once more, I started to seek God about what was next. Much had happened. Many dreams had been fulfilled, and I pondered when more might be fulfilled. I had stopped preaching in high schools, feeling that this was a season of just *prayer*, though I did make occasional stops at clubs I had been a part of.

People would call me to come preach and I'd have to say, "I can't come. God wants to meet with me." I knew my season of praying and fasting wouldn't be long, but I knew I had to obey fully.

I once heard someone say that he would rather teach one man to pray than a hundred to preach. That couldn't be truer. That season turned into a lifestyle of getting to know God. After two and a half years of preaching in high schools, God showed me in those six months of travel and prayer the next piece of the puzzle for seeing every high school saved.

It happened one night as I was praying with a number of people in the Bay area. There was one more One Voice Prayer Gathering scheduled after that one. As I was praying the same prayers I had been speaking for the last few years, God spoke to me.

He reminded me of a dream I'd had one night two years prior. I didn't understand why God was bringing this to mind, since the dream had made no sense, and I had put it on the shelf of my heart.

That dream was now the subject of much talk with God. But what did the number "323," a Hispanic kid and red roofs have to do with where Jesus would take me next?

9

THE "323" DREAM

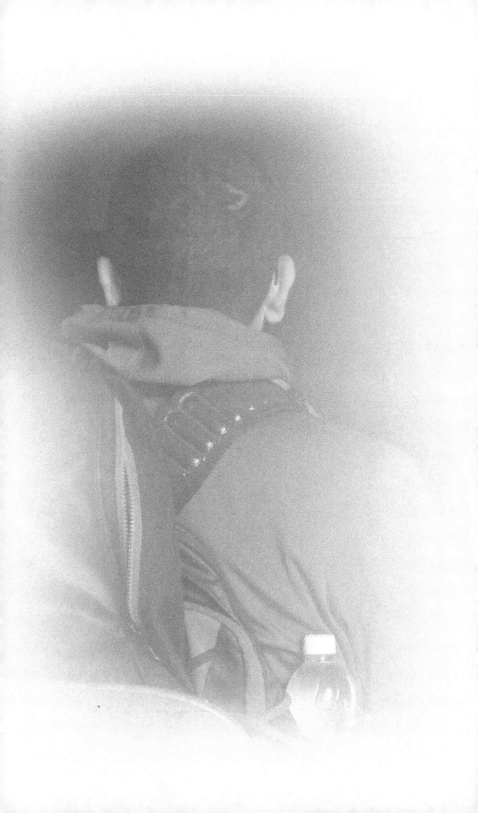

T WAS JUNE 15, 2012, WHEN I MOVED TO Los Angeles. I was seeking a great move of God based on something I had dreamed.

When the Lord first reminded me of this dream, I thought it meant absolutely nothing—but I couldn't get it out of my head. And as I kept pondering it, the idea of going to L.A. began to excite me. As I drove down the long Highway 99, leaving everything behind, I could sense that something was about to happen on the campuses there. I even dreamed of one day marrying the girl in L.A. I had begun to fall in love with named Marcela.

I spent the first month getting settled. A family from a church I had connected with in Northridge called Houses of Light had taken me in. I had just finished preaching there and did what I often did in services: I asked everyone to come forward and pray with me for revival in Los Angeles and for high schools there to be saved.

I felt a lot of hunger in the room and much faith to pray. What I didn't know was that I was about to meet the first person who would join me in this dream of

God for revival in the schools. He also would become a covenant brother and partner.

As several people came to the altar, I began to cry out to the Lord and asked those gathered to pray out loud with me. Allan was one of the first people to respond. I could sense right away that this guy was passionate about God. I could hear him pray over everyone else.

I thought to myself, *This is a guy that I would like to run with*.

The Holy Spirit had spoken to me about Allan in the service that night, so I went to him and told him briefly what I had seen in the schools of Northern California. I then asked if he would meet with me the next day. I knew that I wanted to give him an invitation that I believed would change the course of both our lives.

We met just before lunchtime at our church. The kids' building offered a lot of classrooms that we could use to talk, so we chose a spot, settled in, and I asked Allan to tell me his story. He began to pour out the details of his life, telling me how God had saved him from drugs and a broken family.

He's a perfect candidate for revival, I thought.

Then the conversation grew silent as we both sat there wondering where this was leading. That's when I asked him the question that would change Allan's life and mine.

"Will you run with me in pursuing revival in Los Angeles high schools?" I said.

Allan grew quiet, as if trying to wrap his mind around the question.

"Look," I continued, "the road isn't glamorous but it is glorious. What are you doing right now with your life?"

"School and work and church," he said.

I knew it was time to ask him to give up things I had given up to see God move.

"Allan," I said, leaning forward in my chair, "I want to be up front with you. If you come with me you will have to leave your mom's house and school and work so we can go full-time in this. But I promise we will see a great move of God come to these schools."

It was as though there was an actual weight in the room. It was Allan's moment, the same one I had experienced when God first sent me out to the high schools of America. The fact that God wasn't speaking directly to Allan as He had to me didn't change the weight of the moment or the invitation God was extending.

"Can I think about it?" he said.

"Sure," I answered. "Take three days. But then I'll need an answer."

As he rose to leave, I stopped him and said, "Hey, Allan, I have a meeting tomorrow with Pastor Netz and Lou Engle. Why don't you join me?"

With a smile on his face he said, "I'll be there."

The next day after running a few errands I arrived at the meeting, excited to see my pastor, Netz Gomez, and Lou. As I introduced Allan to Lou I forgot all about the three days I had given him to think about my invitation.

Out of my mouth came the words, "Hey, Lou, I want to introduce you to my new assistant, Allan."

Allan and I both laughed, and then he turned to Pastor Netz, and said, "What do you think?"

Pastor Netz smiled and nodded his head. "Go, son," he said.

This was the start of our One Voice Student Missions community.

In July, Allan and I moved into a two-bedroom guest home that a woman from the church offered me. She told me that the Lord had said to let me live there for free. It had been under construction for months and was finished right around the time we moved.

That was not only home to Allan and me, but it was also our office. This is how One Voice Student Missions began in Los Angeles: me, Allan, not much money and no contacts with any high schools.

But we had faith that Jesus was going to open doors no one else could. It was here that we began to pray for revival and hold meetings with young people from our church to cry out to God to save the high schools of Los Angeles.

About this time, I was asked to help mobilize another prayer event that was going to take place in Pasadena in September with Lou Engle's ministry, TheCall. Marcela was heading up this particular outreach—TheCall Aviva—and they were about to go across California with various tour stops leading to the massive event in September 2012. I jumped at the opportunity, not knowing it would finally begin to connect all the pieces. With high school campuses on my mind and heart, and the odd "323" dream still floating around in my head, nothing about this season I was in made a lot of sense.

Coming to one of the last tour stops with TheCall in August, I found myself at the Hollywood House of Prayer, known now as Radiance House of Prayer, led by a man named Jonathan Ngai. I began talking with Jonathan about all I had seen in Northern California in the high schools.

He told me that he had heard of me and wanted to share something about a high school in Los Angeles called Roosevelt. But before he could say more, I asked if I could tell him something that I had dreamed. I had not shared this dream with anyone, but for some reason I wanted to tell him. I began to describe with as much detail as I could what I had dreamed that summer two years before.

In the dream I was sitting in the back row of a classroom I did not recognize. I was in the second to last seat all the way to the right.

I knew two things while dreaming that night: (1) I wasn't in Northern California and (2) I was not a student. I don't know if that makes sense, but in certain dreams you just know things, and this was one of those times.

As my dream continued, the teacher was talking and the bell was about to ring. As it did, the students and I stood up to leave the classroom. We all headed toward the door and no one seemed to notice me until I walked past the last desk in the right back corner.

At that point, this Hispanic kid grabbed my arm and said to me, "Can I have your phone number?"

I was surprised at this question but without hesitation said yes.

He took out a piece of paper and a pen and wrote down the area code "323." Then he waited for me. I knew he thought I was from that area, wherever that was.

I looked at him and said, "Oh, no, I'm not from here. I'm from Northern California."

He quickly crossed out "323" and wrote "916," my real area code. I gave him the rest of my phone number and left the classroom.

Walking down the stairs of the two-story building, I headed toward the quad, following the kids in front of me. I passed so many students walking around the quad that I figured it must be lunchtime. I wandered aimlessly, not knowing where I was headed but feeling as though I had somewhere to be.

As I walked in the quad I noticed that the buildings had red roofs. A structure with a red canopy stood in the middle of the quad. I made my way eventually to that large room. It was not a gym or auditorium, but I knew students were waiting there for me to preach.

I started to preach and the glory of God came down on that campus. And students started to get saved.

When I woke I was startled—and puzzled. I grabbed my cell phone, struggling to read it, as my eyes were not yet adjusted to the light. I brought up Google and typed "323 area code."

"Los Angeles, California" came up.

A little lost at what this meant and also dealing with the fact that it was six in the morning, I told myself while falling back to sleep, *I will never go to Los Angeles.* Because I could not understand it, I put the dream on the shelf of my heart, basically trying to ignore it from 2010 till now. But I knew the dream had meaning.

As I told Jonathan the dream that evening, he looked at me and began to tell me about Roosevelt High School. He said that about a month before, he had received a prophetic word that God was going to use him and his wife to shut down the first Planned Parenthood clinic on a high school campus, which was Roosevelt. I was captivated. I mean, a school with a Planned Parenthood clinic right on the school grounds was unheard of.

He grabbed his phone and said, "Brian, wouldn't this be crazy if Roosevelt High was in the '323' area code, like in your dream?"

I was nodding as his fingers typed in the information and hit search.

The high schools with area code "323" came up, and the list included Roosevelt High.

A sense of excitement filled me. I had obeyed more than a notion to move to Los Angeles; I was truly on assignment. We began checking details of the school and found out it was in East Los Angeles.

As we read more we found out that this campus was primarily Hispanic. This was also interesting considering that in my dream a Hispanic student had grabbed my arm and asked me for my phone number.

But what did this all mean?

Jonathan and I could not answer that question, so I was left to ponder it. As I prayed I remembered that Paul followed a vision: Acts 16 tells how he saw a vision one night of a man begging him to come to Macedonia. And because Paul followed his vision, he was used by the Holy Spirit to affect the direction of the spread of the Gospel. Because of a dream and one man's willingness to give his life to follow it, the Gospel went west. Could it be that God was divinely using my dream to summon me to the high schools of Los Angeles? And specifically to Roosevelt High? Was the Hispanic student my Macedonian man?

This was all foreign to me. I was not used to getting dreams of this sort. Still, that conversation with Jonathan never left my mind. About a month later I was heading for my car one evening and a few friends asked me where I was going. I told them I was going to the school that Jonathan had told me about, so they piled in, too.

We drove for almost fifty minutes, and for most of that time the words *Am I crazy?* played in my head. But the dots connected so well.

We arrived at Roosevelt High, which was in a rundown neighborhood that looked to be mostly Hispanic. As I pulled up to the curb, I saw that the giant front metal gate was open. I parked the car, and we got out and walked through the gate. It was almost eight o'clock now, and I doubted the school would be open, but it was worth a shot.

As we got closer we were surprised to find that the entrance to the campus was open. We walked in very quietly and made our way through the doorway into the quad.

I couldn't believe my eyes.

There before me was a two-story building with a red roof, and a structure with a red canopy filled the middle of the quad. Everything that I had dreamed two years earlier was right there. The campus was familiar because I had seen it before. I began to tell the guys the significance of that moment.

I walked around the quad a little more and then started up the stairway to the left that led to the doorway of that large building. It was getting darker now, with only a few lights burning from the school's light post. Then God spoke to me again in that familiar voice.

With every step closer to the building in front of me, I heard the Lord say, *Brian, go to those doors; they will be open. Inside there is where you will hold your meetings.*

My meetings? I thought. *What does that mean? Does it mean have a Jesus Club meeting?*

I didn't doubt God could save kids through Jesus Club meetings, but there was one problem. I had no connection with this school at all.

I called down to the guys, "Come on up here."

I thought to myself, *There is no way this building is open after hours.*

When we reached the top of the steps leading away from the quad, I realized that the building was the gym. I grabbed the handle expecting to pull it and feel the jolt of the lock, but to my surprise it swung open. As we walked inside the first thing that hit me was the smell. I knew this definitely was a gym! We made it past the first two doors into the middle room, which had one more pair of doors leading into the main gym.

As I went to open the second pair of doors, my heart was beating fast. I was hoping I wouldn't get into trouble and was not sure what would happen next. My eyes were instantly drawn to the bright colors—yellows and reds—all around. And the huge name on the right side of the wall: Roosevelt High School.

What was going on? How was this all possible?

God spoke to me again, saying that this place would be filled with students getting saved.

After some moments we left, fearing that someone would see us and think we were up to no good.

As we made our way toward the football field, I asked the guys for some time alone. I walked ahead of them out toward the middle of the field. I began to cry, thinking about all that God had spoken to me and shown me.

There was no doubt in my mind or heart that this was the campus I had dreamed of. The fact that I was here was a miracle. There was no way I could have done this on my own.

What amazed me even more, though, was the love God had for this campus. The love He had was so fierce that He gave a man a dream and then placed that man on the campus he had dreamed of.

But He also gave that man a choice to say yes or no.

On that night, standing in the dark, empty football field, I said yes.

Yes to the possibility of God being glorified on this campus.

Yes to souls being saved.

Yes to revival in Los Angeles High Schools.

We left shortly after. I didn't know how I would ever actually get into this school to speak. But my job was done. I was in Los Angeles and had found the school.

The rest was up to God.

10

GOD, IF YOU'RE REAL, TOUCH ME

HAVE MENTIONED THAT A LOT OF KIDS have trouble believing in God, or believing that He is good, because they have never seen anyone model the life of Jesus for them. I knew this would be the case in Los Angeles because it is true in so many lives. It was true in mine.

My younger brother, Joshua, and I were very small when my dad and mom left the Church. I was convinced that God must not be real, because if He was real, why would people leave Him? In our very dysfunctional home, the only sign of faith I saw was from my grandma, who took care of us most of the time because my dad worked so much. She would often take me with her to the church her father had started.

I will never forget the many times I spent the night at my grandma's house and woke to the sound of her praying for me. See, her father and mother (Grandpa and Grandma Mendez) were pastors and church planters. I guess you can say that ministry was in my blood but I wanted nothing to do with religion.

By the time I was fifteen, I was a professing atheist. I couldn't understand any possible reason for people to believe in a God they could not see. When my parents divorced—I was around the age of ten—my life led slowly into depression and anger. And there was no way God could be real.

As young kids, Joshua and I grew up living with our father. I found myself being attracted to the wrong crowds—not because of what they would do but because of the family life they seemed to have. Although my dad did his best to raise us, I felt a God-sized hole in my heart. Not knowing what it was, I tried to fill it with the gangs and any sort of crowd in which I could feel accepted and loved and important.

I longed to be part of a family. I always wondered if there could be more to life.

It was 2005 when, by a divine act of God, I moved in with my mom, whom I had not seen or talked to in four years. I was now fifteen and had a lot going on in my life. Being so confused and broken, I just wanted love. I felt that much of what had happened to me and my family was my fault. I wanted to know my role and my purpose. The many memories of hurt and pain as a kid—seeing my parents constantly fighting—made me feel extremely insecure. I didn't trust very many people. I got firmer in my belief that no God of love existed, let alone loved me.

As time went by I knew there was more to life, but I never knew what it was. It was while living with my mom in Elk Grove that I started pursuing my passion for guitar playing. I stopped all my friendships with gangs and started over, feeling that I could have a fresh start. By the time I was sixteen, I was playing with different shows in bars and nightclubs. They would let me in to play and then kick me out right after, but, hey, it was a show, and I was on my way to getting famous, or so I thought.

In the summer of 2007, Mom and I walked into a grocery store to do our weekly shopping. As we were strolling down the aisles looking for something for dinner, a man spoke our names.

"Brian? Thamar?"

"Beto!" we both said.

Beto, also known as Albert, was an old family friend who lived in the Bay area close to where I had lived with my dad.

For the next few minutes, we caught up on how our families were doing. When he asked me what I was doing in Elk Grove, I explained how I had moved in with my mom, leaving out many details.

"Well, that's amazing!" he said. "How old are you now? What are you doing these days?"

"Well, I'm going to be seventeen soon," I said. "And I've started pursuing my love for music."

Albert started to speak to us about the Lord and about his church. I smiled politely, hiding the fact that I didn't believe in God and really didn't care much for what Beto was saying. As far as I was concerned, I had heard it all before. I had seen too much hypocrisy.

I was only half-listening to this old family friend but heard Albert ask me for my number.

I gave it to him, acting as though it wasn't important, but a part of me was excited that someone wanted to stay connected with me. He kept talking about Jesus and his youth group, and I started to remember the voice of my praying grandma.

"You need Jesus, *hijo*," she used to say. "You need to give your life to Him or else you will go to hell."

Not the most inspiring message, but definitely one I didn't forget. Whenever I tell this story to people I say jokingly that God saw to it I got saved because He must have grown tired of hearing my grandma praying. She was like the persistent widow.

Over the next few months Albert called me several times. He would invite me to church and also to hang out with him. I always found an excuse, but, like Grandma, he was persistent. He invited me to church over and over. And over and over I said no.

I don't know if deep down inside I was truly scared of how real this guy was. I couldn't find much that he did wrong, or anything that proved my case that all Christians were hypocrites. But as the few months passed, my hope was growing darker. Thoughts of suicide often came to mind. I had nothing to live for. I probably looked all right on the outside, but on the inside I was depressed and hopeless.

I finally had to tell Albert straight.

"Look," I said, "I don't do the Jesus thing. I don't do this religious thing. I don't go to church."

With great love he looked at me and said, "Well, I'm not religious either. I have a *relationship* with Jesus." And once again he would invite me to church.

What I realize now looking back is that Albert wasn't inviting me to a service or to a church. He was inviting me to know Jesus.

One day Albert called and said, "We're having a special service tonight, and I want to invite you. If you come tonight, I will buy you a Jamba Juice."

I recalled something that my mother had told me years earlier when I was a kid: "Whatever you can get for free, get it. And try to get some for the family." This was the worst and funniest advice I ever got! But I took it. With my mother's words ringing in my ears, I agreed to go to church.

I planned to go, sit through the hour-and-a-half service, get my Jamba Juice and be done with it. How bad could it be? I'd be in and out, I told myself.

The drive was the most interesting part because, although I didn't want to be there, something in me believed that this night would be different. I somehow knew in my heart that after this night I would never be the same.

When we got to the church I was greeted with smiles by the people at the front door—the people called ushers— and I made my way to the back where I felt most safe. I hoped that if I sat that far back, no one would notice me.

I was totally disengaged from the presence of God. Yet God was in hot pursuit of my heart. In that moment, I believe the Holy Spirit was closer than ever. Even now writing this I am in tears realizing how the love of God draws in and invites His sons and daughters to know Him.

I watched the people in the front of the church dance and jump as kids my age played worship songs. Those kids looked crazy to me.

They must be on drugs, I thought. *What possesses them to look so foolish? Why are they looking so happy?*

But the more I observed, the more I realized that the kids were expressing the inward joy they felt. It was a joy I had never experienced but one that I couldn't deny they had.

What do they have that I don't? I wondered.

With my arms crossed, I looked up toward the ceiling and spoke to a God I didn't believe was there.

They're saying You're the King of kings, I said, forming the words in my mind. *They're saying You died on a cross and rose from the dead.*

With anger in my heart, I understood for the first time the repressed hurt I had from my parents leaving the Church. I knew that I had blamed Him for their divorce and my brokenness. I felt that God in so many ways had left me and let me down.

At that point I felt I had nothing to lose. God wasn't real anyway, and this was my way to prove that once and for all.

But as I kept talking, various things my grandma had told me about Jesus started to come into my mind. A spiritual inheritance—birthed in me from all the people who had spoken the Word of God into my life—came alive that very moment. It is funny how the seeds people sow can in one moment break ground and sprout.

"Jesus, I don't know if You're real," I said. "But if You are, I dare You to touch me."

Suddenly, I felt supernatural power come over my body. I know now it was the Holy Spirit coming upon me. From the top of my head to the bottom of my feet, I felt Love come over me. The chains I had carried spiritually began to break off me—chains of depression, chains of suicide, chains of bitterness, chains of resentment, chains of anger, chains of lust.

I started weeping uncontrollably. I was literally sobbing, gripped by love. I couldn't see the freedom I was experiencing, but I could feel it in my heart and soul. It was an amazing love that I had never felt before in my life. This love was the gentlest type of love, yet it was fierce. God had waited sixteen years for me to say those words, words that gave Him permission to touch my heart. He had longed not only for me to go to heaven but for Him to put heaven in me.

A friend of mine, Todd White, often says to me, "Heaven went bankrupt to get us!" That day the payment for my life was received. I felt the touch of freedom for the first time ever. The battle between darkness and light was about to be over. I was coming into the light.

Albert came up to me, grabbed my shoulders and asked me if I wanted to go up front and receive Jesus. Without waiting for a response, he started to guide me to the front.

Looking back on it now, all I can say is that when bold love grips your heart, you respond. And that's what I did that night.

A woman on the stage spoke into the mic in her hand for all to hear.

"Would you like to accept Jesus into your heart?" she asked.

Tears flooded my eyes and, as I nodded my head, I heard the students cheering for joy. They knew more about the decision I was making than I did.

With my eyes closed, I prayed the prayer of salvation, asking Jesus Christ to come into my heart. Asking Him to be my *Lord* and *Savior*. My King forever.

But it was more than a prayer. It was a vow to follow Jesus the rest of my life. It was a yes to my generation. It was the yes for me to fight for the freedom of those who can't fight for themselves.

It was a yes to go when and where Jesus would tell me.

I don't believe that a prayer alone secures a spot in heaven that can never be lost. I believe that salvation prayer is the wedding of a marriage that must be walked out. Many get married; few stay married. And deep in my heart I knew that this decision was for life.

When I opened my eyes after praying, everything looked different. I mean, everything! I felt as if darkness had been shattered off my eyes. I am serious when I say that I could see for the first time in my sixteen years. I could breathe. I could live. The devil had lost his grip on my life.

In that one moment, depression and pain were broken from me. And I truly believe that as the angels rejoiced over my name being written in the Lamb's Book of Life, so hell trembled at what God would do through my life. Only the Lord knew I would grow up and not keep this light to myself. Looking back it makes sense why the enemy likes to try to keep us from knowing who we are in Christ.

I was changed. No longer an atheist who denied Jesus, I was now a Christian who would do nothing but love God and love the people I encountered.

God had set me up with a promise of a Jamba Juice. No one was more surprised than I was.

While I was still at the front of the church, the students gathered around me and hugged me, celebrating that I had come to Christ. Finally I understood their jumping, their shouting and their laughing. My existence made sense. My life would no longer be my own.

As we drove home, Albert and I talked the whole time about how things had changed. I felt I owed him for what had happened. But he would always point me back to Christ.

"Well, I'll see you next week, right?" he said, when we got to my house.

"Yes!" I exclaimed. "Of course!"

I ran to the house, unlocking the door and trying not to make too much noise. I wasn't sure if my mom and stepdad and brother and sister were asleep, as it was a little late. I couldn't wait to tell them of my experience, although I didn't know how they would react.

As I closed the door to my room, I looked around and saw things I now wanted to get rid of. I started to throw everything away.

I asked myself, *If Jesus walked into my room, what would offend Him? What would hurt His heart?*

No one gave me a sheet of directions about what to do as a new believer. There was no Discipleship 101 class or book given to me that night. I simply had a conviction in my heart about what is right and what is wrong. God had gloriously and mysteriously awakened something inside me.

I realized that there are two types of people: those who get saved and those who get *really* saved. While many of the saved ones go back to living life the way they were before, those who get *really* saved can never live life the same again.

I'm not speaking of struggling with things you are overcoming; I'm speaking of going back. Knowing the truth and not caring to follow it. When we truly taste and see the Lord we cannot help but want more.

Conviction was within my heart, and love fueled my decisions. I threw away posters, CDs, books and a box of pornography. I was done with the filth.

That night was the beginning of the rest of my life.

Still, to this day, although I have seen gyms and auditoriums full of students who want to hear about Jesus, and have seen God save thousands, heal hundreds and invade innumerable people's lives with love, nothing has felt like that day when darkness fled my soul and light invaded my heart.

And oh, what a joy it is to see that same thing happen to others!

This is what drives me to schools every week. This is what drives me to intercede for God to save the high schools of America and restore prayer there.

I did realize one other thing as God prepped me for my work in Roosevelt High and other schools in Los Angeles: Jesus is worthy of every heart in every school in every state in the nation.

My goal in sharing my story is not to look back on a joyful experience so I can remember a good time; my goal is to see others have the same one.

11

FOLLOW ME

ONE NIGHT AS I SAT IN MY ROOM IN the little house in Sylmar where Allan and I lived, I remember thinking, *God, is anything ever going to happen in L.A.?*

We had been praying for months but were seeing almost no results. I heard myself asking God if He was ever going to use me again. Maybe He had guided me in Elk Grove but was done with me.

I heard His voice speak firmly: *Get up.*

I stood and said out loud, "Yes, Jesus?"

Somehow I kind of knew what He was going to say. *Ask Me.*

"Ask You what, God?"

Ask Me to save the high schools of Los Angeles, and I will do it.

My heart was instantly filled with faith. I had such godly confidence that no matter what it looked like on the outside I knew I had God's backing. I began to pace back and forth in my room, asking the Lord once again to save the high schools of Los Angeles. That room became my prayer closet as Allan and I took hold of God's promise.

As more weeks passed, many people in our church and other friends thought we were crazy. I mean, normal people our age were pursuing education or careers. We were praying. Actually, what many of them didn't understand was that we *were* pursuing careers: careers in missions. And, no, we didn't have paychecks coming in, but we had a word from the Lord. And we were two covenant brothers who dared to believe it.

The mission field was before us; we didn't have to go far to find it. It was clear what God was asking. I started to preach in small churches throughout L.A., sharing stories of what had happened in Northern California, provoking others to believe the same could happen here.

Little by little other young people from our church were attracted to the mission and joined us. I am in no way against college or working a nine-to-five job, but I am 100 percent for obeying God. I believe that some young people are in college whom God has called to the mission field and some young people are on the mission field whom God has called to college. And I also believe that, for some, college is their mission field.

All I am saying is that obeying God comes before all. And this was a great testing of our hearts. The fact that many church leaders didn't understand it, didn't mean that God wasn't in it.

As momentum was picking up in early 2013, I had a meeting in our little house. I invited a few people I thought would answer the call just as Allan had. These were people who had ministered with me in a few places and who, I knew, had a heart of love for others.

I invited them to come, saying I would cook dinner. Then I remembered I couldn't cook and went out and bought sandwiches.

Free food is free food, I thought.

I did, however, set the table and prepare for a night that, I felt, could change their lives.

Though they laughed when I brought out the dinner I had "cooked," they grew serious with interest as I began to describe what I had heard God saying and the plans I believed He had for One Voice Student Missions. At the end, I gave them the same invitation I had given Allan.

The silence that followed was broken by a few yeses and also a few nos. One girl named Lily agreed to set aside her schooling for a while and pioneer with us. Little did she know that she, too, would be part of a longer journey than she probably ever imagined.

One Voice now had two campus missionaries besides myself—Allan and Lily—and we knew one thing: God had promised to save the schools of Los Angeles.

Soon after that meeting, Lou Engle invited me to speak at Mott Auditorium, a well-known place in Pasadena where many would gather weekly to hear Lou share about revival and prayer. He wanted to hear more about what God was doing through One Voice. This truly was an honor for me.

After I spoke, Lou asked those present to lay hands on me and pray that God would make me a sign and wonder to America.

During that prayer, one of the guys from the Circuit Riders prophesied: "The Lord says that one hundred thousand high school students in Los Angeles, California, will be saved."

My heart leapt with joy at that word. It was one of many confirmations that we were on the right track.

Over the next few months, others answered God's call to join us and pursue the salvation of high school students. Elisabeth had come to America from Germany because of a word from God that Hollywood would be saved. She joined us after hearing me that night at Mott. Another girl named Soyoon, who was Korean, also joined.

We now had five including me. It was time to have our first real One Voice meeting to define what exactly we were committing ourselves to. I was never one to organize teams, but I knew it was crucial to be strategic so that time wouldn't be wasted.

I had transformed my bedroom into an office, taking out my bed and bringing in a flag and a desk and a futon that gave me back problems every day. We met there and made the commitment to embrace a lifestyle based on Psalm 110:3, which says that in the day of the power of the Lord, His people will offer their lives freely.

Together, we said yes, making a covenant commitment for two years—not knowing that we would give many more. Our commitment was to give ourselves freely to the work of reaching high schools, and to consider it our joy to do all God was asking us to do.

Ultimately, we decided to give our lives for the high schools of America. And as the verse said, we would do so voluntarily.

It wasn't for fame or money. We certainly didn't have much of either—only the stories of what God had done and the faith of what we knew He was going to do. We didn't need the security of regular paychecks, although we welcomed any financial partnerships that came to us to help us reach schools.

We were doing it because we believed God wanted to save the schools. And the Lamb of God is worthy of the reward of His sufferings.

Within a few months, the office for our growing team moved from the guesthouse to a small room in our church in Northridge. When Pastor Netz found out where we were meeting, he offered us room in the church to use. We were very grateful. The room was small, but so were our small beginnings.

That room became the headquarters for One Voice, the place where we would pray and plan how to spread the Good News. I took all the money I had to my name and bought desks and a few other basic supplies, trying to make our office feel a little more legit.

Allan, Lily, Elisabeth, Soyoon and I all shared a heart for revival. We would talk all the time about what God wanted to do. And we would ponder how we were going to fund the ministry.

I commended these people all the time, because it is one thing to serve a ministry that is flourishing, but few can pioneer moves of God with committed hearts when little fruit is seen.

During this time, I received a call from Lou Engle's assistant. He asked me to do a favor and give an elderly woman known as Grandma Willi a ride to Pasadena for an event being held there.

I didn't know her but, wanting to serve, I was honored to pick her up. I showed up at her home, got out of my car, walked up the steps and knocked on the door. It opened, and there stood the kindest woman I had ever met.

I helped her down the stairs and into the car and we were off. As we drove to Pasadena, we began to talk and things clicked. This was the woman Lou often described as he preached who had funded the first historic Call event in the year 2000 where 470,000 gathered in Washington, D.C.

What an honor to be with her, I thought, but tried to keep my cool knowing I was sitting with a legend.

When we arrived, she went inside and was escorted from there by people from TheCall's team. Once the event was over, she rejoined me for the ride back to her home.

As we began to drive, her head started to nod in sleep. I knew she had had a long day, and, after all, she was 89 years old.

Before she closed her eyes, she said to me, "So what do you *do*?"

I began to tell her about the experiences in Northern California and the thousands of students who had received Jesus.

She sat up straighter and said, "Tell me more."

So I told her everything—how God had given me a promise, and how I had dreamed about coming to L.A., and how we now had a team that was going after high schools for Jesus.

She didn't say much until we pulled up to her house. Then she said words that I will never forget.

"You know," she said, "thirteen years ago I met a man I knew would change the destiny of America. His name is Lou Engle. But I have not met another man like that until today, when I met you."

Not knowing what to say I put my head down, thinking of all the reasons I was not a man to change anything.

Then she said she believed that what we were doing was the answer to saving America.

"I want to talk to you more," she said. "Please give me a call tomorrow."

As I walked her to her door, I once again felt God's hand on my life. He was not just leading me, but connecting me with key people who were part of His plan to reach high schools.

I spoke with Grandma Willi several times after that. She began not just to encourage us, but also to help our ministry financially.

I truly can say that when I am 89 years old, I want to be just like her. I want to be a person who gives generously to see the next generation reached.

Through Grandma Willi's generosity and the obedience of the One Voice team, God was about to make a historic visit to the high schools of Los Angeles.

12

GOD LOVES LAUSD

WE HAD, BY THE GRACE OF GOD, made connections over the previous months with a few campuses in the Los Angeles Unified School District. Chatsworth High and El Camino High, in the Valley, and Fairfax High near Hollywood were among the first campuses to open to us.

Week after week I traveled with our team to the Jesus Clubs at these schools to preach the Gospel. It had been about a year now since my friends and I had visited Roosevelt High that night when God had said He would fill the gym. And, actually, my heart and mind were still fixed on God moving there. I knew it held significance for all the L.A. schools.

If that "Goliath" (Roosevelt High School) came down, a nation of high schools would get faith again.

I asked God over and over, "Is this still what You want to do?"

And the only response I got was encouragement to be faithful. I was doing that to the best of my ability.

Yet, still, no door opened into Roosevelt. I was practically pounding on the chest of God in prayer, asking Him to give us entry. I was trying to find students who went there—or knew someone who did—but everything was a dead end.

I was invited at one point to a small, Spanish-speaking church, and Allan went with me along with a few others. My words had to be translated, since I don't know Spanish. I poured out my heart for revival, pausing along the way for the translator. Speaking with a translator was never my favorite, as I felt my passion being put on hold for a three-second delay. I was hoping the people in the little church could hear how desperately we needed to reach the L.A. high schools.

As the service was coming to a close, I asked the congregation to join me in crying out to God for revival. Then, as we finished, I thanked the pastor who had invited me and headed to my car to wait for the others. I was a little tired after that night.

Sitting there, I saw a man walk up to Allan. He looked to be a little over six feet tall and was all tatted up. I could tell this man had had some connection with gangs, and I wondered what he was saying to Allan.

Then, with a huge smile, Allan made big gestures with his arm for me to get out of the car and join them. I did so, even though I couldn't imagine what he was so excited about.

Then the man repeated to me what he had just said to Allan.

"I heard you guys are trying to get into Roosevelt High."

"Yes!" I exclaimed.

I began telling him of our dreams, all that God had spoken.

"We've been trying to get into Roosevelt for almost a year," I said. "We've not had any success or made any connections."

"Well," he said, "I'm a drug and alcohol counselor at Roosevelt High School. I didn't know why I was assigned to that school until I heard you speak tonight. I want to help you guys get on campus."

I couldn't believe it. I was beyond shocked. I mean, this was the kind of stuff I had only heard other people talk about. Out of all the places I had preached, God used this small church to provide a contact who would be the key to our getting into a school that would make history for high school movements.

Repentance hit my heart as I realized once again that I don't always understand God's ways. In the most unlikely place, He had provided exactly what we needed.

We exchanged phone numbers. He said that he would find the student who led the Bible club at Roosevelt and get me his number. Now, truth be told, I had a moment of doubt that he would actually follow through. Many times in my life people have told me they would do something and it never happened.

But a few days later, my phone rang and it was the counselor. I was amazed when he said that he had hunted down the student and his name was Uriel.

"Did you get his number?" I asked.

"Yes and he is waiting for your call."

I thanked him and dialed Uriel's number quickly, thinking that this student leader would either think I was crazy or join us and believe for God to save his campus.

After three rings a voice said, "Hello?"

My heart paused for a brief half a second as I cleared my throat to speak.

"Hi, my name is Brian Barcelona from One Voice," I said. "You don't know me, but I promise I'm not crazy."

I know it wasn't the best opening line for meeting someone on the phone, but it was all I had.

I proceeded to tell the story to Uriel of all that had happened in the Jesus Clubs in Northern California, sharing the growth of our meetings and the miracles we had seen. I hoped it would be enough for him to understand my heart and passion for high schools.

Then, without hesitation, I moved on to the dream about the Hispanic kid and the red roofs in a school with a "323" area code, and how I had been praying for a year to get into Roosevelt.

The phone went silent. I could feel my heart pounding. Then he spoke.

"I must work with you," Uriel said.

"Why do you say that?" I asked. I was surprised that he was so responsive so quickly.

"A few months ago," Uriel explained, "my mother came home from a conference and told me about a man working in high schools and that his name was Brian Barcelona."

"Really?" I said. Inside I was freaking out that he was saying this.

"I've been trying to reach the guy running One Voice, but I couldn't get ahold of him," he said. "Now you call me on my phone. I must work with you."

There have been moments in my walk with God when I am left completely in awe. This was one of those.

Oh, how God orchestrates His plans and will for our lives!

"Yes," I said. "We have to meet—and before this next school year starts."

I drove out once again to East L.A. to Roosevelt, down those busy streets, not knowing that this would be my weekly routine for the next years to come.

But this time things were completely different.

I met Uriel in front of the school since classes were not in session. I could tell right away that he was powerful in his love and zeal for God. We walked a block down the street toward a café to meet with another Bible club student named Mishael. Uriel told me that the café was owned by Roosevelt graduates and was well-known in the community.

We opened the squeaky glass door and walked inside. After he introduced me to Mishael, we got a table, ordered our food and began to talk about all we wanted to do at Roosevelt that year. As I shared more and more stories, tears began to fill their eyes.

I turned to Uriel.

"I believe you're the kid from my dream," I told him. "And your school is on the heart of God to be saved. If you will work with me, I believe we will see a great move of God come to this campus."

He and Mishael agreed that this was God's leading. They wanted to work with me. We didn't know what it would look like, or how we would reach the whole school, but at least we had an opening.

After our meeting, Uriel, Mishael and I spent the summer planning and dreaming for their school. On many days our whole team would eat and talk and pray together for God to move powerfully.

As the opening of school approached, all was in place. The Jesus Club leaders were ready and filled with faith. And we had connected with the teacher sponsor of the Jesus Club that year, Mr. Sam Alba.

Finally the day came for us to be on the school grounds during lunchtime. I walked around, just checking out the campus and feeling that my dream was becoming more and more real.

And faith grew in my heart as well. I saw the gangs and jocks and the different groups of kids who didn't hang out together. My heart broke as I looked past the name-brand clothes, past the cliques, and saw into the brokenness—not only of this school, but of this whole generation.

The next week our One Voice team held our first meeting with the Roosevelt High Jesus Club. We gathered in a second-story classroom that looked similar to the one in my dream.

The first part of the dream—me sitting in this classroom on the second story of this building in this high school—was fulfilled; the salvation part was yet to come.

Six students came to that meeting. I told them that God was about to do something phenomenal. When I had finished, Mr. Alba came to the front of the room and started to say how this message was from God, and that he was standing with us.

I didn't know until later that Mr. Alba and his cousin Mr. Sam Gamboa were students at Roosevelt High in the 1970s and founded the first Bible club on that campus. Now, almost forty years later, God was allowing this man to see the fruit of their labor.

I believe the faith they had in the 1970s gave a young man in the year 2010 a dream. And that dream would prove to be from God very soon. God honors the covenants and promises He makes. He was doing that very thing in this moment in the classroom.

For now, in the time we had left at this first Jesus Club meeting, we needed to start planning ways to reach the school. We knew that we wanted to meet next in the gym or auditorium, always going for the biggest place we could get.

I had an idea.

"Donuts," I said.

"Donuts?" they said back.

"Yes. This is how we are going to reach this campus."

The word had dropped into my heart. It was as if God had revealed the identity of a secret weapon to win the hearts of students. I mean, who doesn't like a glazed donut?

"Yes," I said, gaining momentum. "For the next two weeks let's meet in the quad, and three weeks from now we'll hold our first Jesus Club meeting in the gym or the auditorium. Let's give out hundreds of donuts and pray for the kids and tell them about Jesus."

Little did I know that donuts would be the basis for building friendships that would last years. Those donuts would allow gang members and drug addicts to become my friends. And through this simple act of love, many would come to know Jesus.

So the next Tuesday we began handing out donuts during lunch. It was so popular that the school paper ran an article called "Food and Faith," actually commending us for coming and giving free food to the students.

In the meantime, Uriel and Mr. Alba worked to get a place for us to meet. The gym was booked for the day we wanted, September 11, but the auditorium, which held sixteen hundred, was wide open. I had passed this auditorium a few times on my way to Mr. Alba's room.

After about a week and a half, Mr. Alba had secured everything. All we had to do now was love people and invite them to come to the lunchtime Jesus Club meeting. As the day drew near, I was excited yet a little afraid. Everything depended on God.

That Wednesday morning, we opened the doors to the large old auditorium building, which had been built in 1923, amazed that we had the faith to believe God would use six students, a teacher and a small team to fulfill His promise for this campus. The auditorium had this old smell, like an antique store. We tidied things up a little, trying to make the room look as attractive as possible.

As the minutes ticked by, we waited eagerly for lunchtime to start. The team got together and prayed, asking God to show up in this meeting.

When the bell rang, my heart paced even harder. One by one students came, pouring by the hundreds into the auditorium. Three hundred, to be exact. This was the moment we had been waiting for. The kids might not have known what they had just walked into, but I knew they would never leave the same.

I started to preach about God's love.

At the start, most of the students were talking to each other, but I kept going. I was used to being interrupted by students. And, of course, this was to be expected. How could I expect students who had never met Jesus to act any other way?

I gave my testimony toward the end of my message. Then, feeling the leading of the Holy Spirit, I shouted, "If you want to encounter the love of God and give your life to Jesus, I don't want you to close your eyes or bow your heads; I want you to stand to your feet. If there were a fight outside, you'd stand on tables to see it. You'd stand for drugs, gangs and sex. Now stand up for something much greater."

I could feel the presence of God so strongly that it seemed as if heaven stood behind me, backing up all I was saying by touching hearts in that auditorium.

As my eyes darted around the room, I saw students begin to rise to their feet. A few and then more and more until every single student was standing, many of them weeping. All three hundred of them answered the call of God to receive His Son, Jesus, into their hearts.

I told them to repeat a prayer with me. It was one I knew very well. I have said it hundreds of times. It was the prayer confessing Jesus as Lord. As three hundred students shouted the words, we felt the grip of hell lose its power over many lives.

The response to that meeting was so dramatic that the administration approached us later and offered the use of the gym to facilitate what we were doing. The promise God gave me a year earlier that the gym would be full of kids was about to come true.

That one meeting in the auditorium sparked a flame. Three weeks later 450 kids piled into the gymnasium for Jesus Club during lunch. Within months Roosevelt High School felt like an Azusa Street revival. As word spread, people from all over the United States and other nations came to see what God was doing.

Over those months, from September to January, we were blown away by what we saw. The toughest students on campus were encountering Jesus. I would often find Mr. Alba in tears after the meetings, amazed at what God was doing.

As our One Voice team and the Jesus Club leaders began to explore the idea of reaching people on campus who weren't coming to the Jesus Club meetings, we came up with the idea of holding an assembly before lunch. That would give us the opportunity to share the love of God with the whole school population.

My team and I believed that, if students came in two groups, we could get all two thousand into one room to hear a message of hope.

Amazingly, through Mr. Alba's guidance and hard work, we received permission from school officials to conduct an assembly sponsored by the Jesus Club during school hours.

This was historic.

We were given the date of February 26. I saw more and more that God truly works everything out for the good of those who love Him.

As we coordinated with the school to plan the event, our biggest question now was whom to get as speaker. We knew it had to be someone who could walk the line of sharing the love of God yet honoring the rare position we were in of holding a Jesus Club assembly during school hours.

And I never would have guessed in a million years who that special person would turn out to be.

13

THE "ABOVE ALL, LOVE" ASSEMBLY

I T WAS JANUARY 2014 AND WE HAD JUST returned from the winter break. We were getting ready to start up our Jesus Club meetings again. Our team was also preparing for another One Voice gathering. We wanted to give leaders and pastors in the city a chance to learn what God was doing in the high schools and to get involved themselves.

I was excited to think about all the people who might possibly join with One Voice through the gathering. But I was even more excited when I received a call from a friend who told me that evangelist Todd White was in town, and that one of his representatives wanted to meet with me to talk about what was going on with us.

I was excited because I had seen Todd give his testimony and teach about power evangelism and street ministry on YouTube years before. I never thought I would have the honor to meet him, let alone become amazing friends.

I would always think to myself, *I wish I could meet this guy*. But truthfully, I never knew how it would happen.

The only time the representative had available happened to be on the same afternoon of our gathering, about two hours before it all started.

"Let's do it," I said, not wanting to miss any opportunity.

That Saturday, my team and I were at the church with about two hours left before the gathering was to start.

While we were talking and laughing, one of the kids helping us ran up to me and said, "Brian! Todd White is here!"

My response was "Stop lying, man!"

"No," he said in a jumble of excitement, "for real! He's here. He has dreadlocks. He's just arrived!"

I thought, *Could it really be Todd White and not just a pastor who has dreads who looks like him?*

I jumped up, heading for the entrance door, my team right behind me. I pulled open the door, looked outside and saw Todd White standing there.

I sprinted down the stairway to him.

"Hello, Todd," I said, extending my hand. "My name is Brian Barcelona." *Excitement* doesn't express how I felt in that moment.

Todd looked past my hand, opened his arms and gave me a hug. In that moment when he hugged me, I felt the love of Jesus I had seen in him on YouTube. I knew from that moment that this guy was crazy legit.

The timing couldn't have been better. As we walked into the church to sit and talk, Brian Brennt and Lou Engle, who were the speakers for our gathering, joined us. For the next hour we talked about all that God was doing in the high schools.

It was an unusual moment. It felt as though all of us had brought our individual histories into that room, and that they were all colliding—as though this was a time and place specially designed by the Lord.

As the conversation was ending, I went over to Todd privately and asked if he would pray for me and my soon-to-be-wife, Marcela. I don't remember what he prayed, but I do remember being touched by God through his prayer.

Then he amazed me even more.

"Brian," he said, "I want to help you in any way I can." He went on to tell me that three years earlier, a prophetic friend of his told him that the next Jesus Movement was going to start in California—in the high schools.

His friend told him that the movement would sweep up and down the state of California, and then go to the East Coast and up through Canada.

The final part of the prophecy was that Todd himself would be a major part of this Jesus Movement.

I stood there speechless.

But I gathered my wits in the few moments I had left with Todd and asked him a question that had been on my mind the whole time we had all been talking.

And that question was this: What if Todd White was supposed to be our guest speaker at the Roosevelt High assembly?

So I asked him.

I told him that we expected all two thousand students to come, but I acknowledged that it was short notice, as the assembly was just a few weeks away—on February 26.

He pulled out his cell phone to check his calendar.

"Looks as though February 26 and 27 are the only days I'm free to come for a while," he said with a smile.

God had once again brought everything together. I knew that the students were going to experience something they had never experienced before. We hugged and parted ways.

Now everything was set.

We worked tirelessly trying to promote the assembly in a non-religious way. We decided to call it "Above All, Love." We passed out flyers and put letters into teachers' mailboxes inviting them.

On the day of the assembly I picked up Todd from the airport and we were on our way. When we arrived at Roosevelt, the team had already started to set up. I was glad that Pastor Netz and Lou were there to witness this, along with many other leaders.

The assembly was broken into two periods of around a thousand students each. The first group was in, and we began.

Sometimes the hardest part of assemblies is getting the students quiet. As I stood to introduce Todd, I saw expressions on their faces that seemed to be saying, "Who is this guy with dreads?"

"Hey, everyone," I began, "I know you may have seen me during your lunch giving out donuts or in the gym."

Getting a few claps and shouts, I continued. "I want to introduce you to my friend Todd White. He wants to share his story with you today. Give it up for Todd White!" I shouted, thinking to myself how rare it was to be saying this in an auditorium of a thousand students.

As Todd took the mic, he did something I never would have expected. He started to beatbox, perfectly swishing and tapping the sound of percussion with his mouth.

I was in no way expecting this. But the kids went crazy. Literally, Todd had earned their respect in about thirty seconds.

Then he began to speak.

"I know you have come to hear my story of how I changed," he said. "But if I tell you a story, then that would imply I changed myself. I want to tell you a testimony."

The auditorium was dead silent. Todd began to talk about his faith in Jesus. I stood there, nervous, not sure how the students or teachers were going to respond—and to my surprise, it was the most well received assembly I had ever been in.

As Todd finished he mentioned that if they wanted to hear the rest of his testimony to come to the gym during lunch. We had a short time between the first and second assemblies, and students and teachers alike lined up in tears to greet him.

When I picked up the mic to open the second assembly, I noticed the principal walking into the room and I hesitated for a moment. This was a school-sponsored event, unlike the other nighttime rallies or lunchtime Jesus Club meetings. I wondered what would happen when the principal heard the name of Jesus being lifted up. Would he be obligated to bring the assembly to a close?

Then I remembered that the principal rapped. I had actually heard him rapping once in the quad with students following on a beatbox.

Without taking time to think, I shouted, "How many would love to hear your principal rap as Todd White beatboxes?"

The room erupted.

The principal smiled and walked to the stage amid the shouts and whistles of the students.

The beatboxing and rapping lasted a couple of minutes, just enough to win the hearts of the students in this second assembly. And I saw that I had nothing to worry about.

Todd again gave his testimony about what God had done in his life. And as with the first assembly, many stayed afterward to speak with him. I spoke into the mic that anyone who wanted to hear more of Todd's story could head to the gym.

I remember very well certain moments in my heart. This was one of those special ones. As Todd and I were walking to the gym, I looked back and saw hundreds of students all around us, following us. Eight hundred students filled the gym that lunchtime, and God began to heal both their hearts and bodies as Todd ministered to them.

What made that day such a one to remember wasn't just that Todd White came to minister or that eight hundred kids gathered in the gym for a Jesus Club meeting. It was that Jesus was made famous to a whole student body.

These rallies and assemblies in gyms and auditoriums were in many ways only the beginning. Our One Voice team started to believe that one day these would be tools to gather masses to Jesus Clubs. And we believed that one day beyond that, we would see a youth revival or crusade begin in the L.A. area. We longed to see students—along with their families—gather. What if fathers and mothers and brothers and sisters got saved as well?

I had learned at this point in my journey that any time wild ideas come into our hearts, it's for sure the devil hasn't given them and our own minds haven't thought them up. It is God who deposits seeds that may take years to grow.

By the end of the 2014 school year, the idea of youth crusades in high schools was a good seed that had begun to take hold and grow. It would not be long until we would see the fruit.

14

THE COST

ONE OF THE REASONS I THINK THE kids at the Roosevelt High assembly were able to respond at such a deep level was Todd's willingness to share with them about some of the hard times in his life—the same as Rev. D. had done at Valley High.

You know, it's easy for many of us today who speak the Good News of Jesus, whether at churches, youth groups, conferences or any other Christian event, to share our amazing victory stories. I'm not saying at all that it is wrong to tell the wild stories of how God showed up. There are many in the Body of Christ who desperately need encouraging stories as fuel to launch them into their destinies.

But sometimes we need just as much to hear about getting through the rough times, the stories where people fell short but overcame.

To be honest, many times I find it hard to open up about the things that have been really difficult. The moments where it wasn't easy, the times where I wanted to quit, the situations where I doubted God would come through.

I have made many mistakes in my walk with God; many times I didn't obey as well as I wanted to. I know that I have hurt people unintentionally in my crazy pursuit for God. I think that if the people who know me were to state all my shortcomings, it could be a book of its own. There have been many moments the Lord asked me to do certain things, and my heart responded no. But through it all, it's never how we start something; it's always how we finish.

If you and I are to run this race in following Jesus, then we must learn one verse from the Bible inside and out. And we truly must not be content with memorizing something we are not living. Quoting Scripture doesn't change a generation; living it does. I know for sure that if the Lord is going to do all He wants to do in our high schools, He needs people who will be 100 percent real about the places He has brought them out of.

Look at this verse:

And He has said to me, "My grace is sufficient for you, for power is perfected in weakness." Most gladly, therefore, I will rather boast about my weaknesses, so that the power of Christ may dwell in me. Therefore I am well content with weaknesses, with insults, with distresses, with persecutions, with difficulties, for Christ's sake; for when I am weak, then I am strong.

2 Corinthians 12:9–10

The moments I feel God's grace, as I pursue what He asks me to do, are times of my greatest weakness. I remember once I preached a message that I had worked on really hard. I had practiced it at home, going over all the points I wanted to hit the next day as I stood before five or six hundred students.

"I Am a Masterpiece" was the name of my message, and I remember wishing I could answer the altar call with the students because I didn't much feel like the masterpiece I was preaching about.

After that Jesus Club meeting I battled with thoughts and feelings that come at me many times. Thoughts like: *My message wasn't good enough; nobody understood it; if the students didn't encounter Jesus, it was my fault.*

See, there is a big problem with all of these lies from hell. Number One, the words I speak are never my messages but God's. Number Two, it's never my job to judge what kind of soil is in the room; it's only my job to shut up and throw seed and let God do the rest. And Number Three, if the students don't encounter Jesus because of me, then when they do encounter Him does it happen because of me?

No! Never.

That particular night I was really discouraged. I went home and spent some time on Facebook. I know I probably should have opened my Bible or gone to my room to pray, but I didn't.

At one point I stumbled onto the pages of students who had actually attended that Jesus Club meeting. They had written testimonies of how God had changed their lives, and many of them now realized they were God's masterpieces.

I began laughing and wondering why I ever allowed those negative thoughts to stay in my heart and mind for so long.

I'm sure some of it came from the fact that I had so few funds and felt so misunderstood in my mission field. The fact that I longed to please God while not truly understanding my sonship didn't help either.

And, besides, how could God use a man with so many imperfections? My years of growing up weren't the easiest. For several years as a young teen in Elk Grove, I never really had a place to call home. From the time my stepdad left three days before Christmas, my mom couldn't afford to take care of my brother and sister and me.

So I had to move out when I was seventeen, some months after I was saved. I spent many nights sleeping on people's floors and couches. Sometimes I was blessed to stay in a host's home until my stay was no longer welcomed. I know this doesn't sound like a success story or even how a Christian should be living. But as Paul says, my strength is in my boasting of my weakness—and my home life was probably the biggest area of weakness.

I wish I could tell you my dad was a strong believer or my mom loved God and lived for Him, but that's just not my story. By the same token, my home life shouldn't be an excuse for failing to pursue God with all I have.

The hardest part of staying with another family is that you never feel as though you are part of it. Thoughts of being a burden would often hit my heart. I can't tell you how many times I had to encourage myself in the Lord to get out of bed and go to the high school where I'd be preaching. I felt like a hypocrite because I was speaking truth that hadn't set my own heart free in certain ways. That's when the verse about God's grace being perfected in my weakness became embedded in my heart and soul. "For when I am weak, then I am strong." The greatest messages I shared were tied in to personal moments of needing God as badly as the people I was preaching to. Sometimes I had to preach truth to others until I started to believe it.

Someone once said you can't have a baby without poop, you can't have a barn without it smelling like a barn, and you can't have revival without some mess. I know that in many ways I could have handled things better. But I have learned, looking back, that everything I go through—whether easy or hard, good or bad—teaches me one thing: to remain steadfast in what God has asked me to do.

The times I fall short remind me of how One Voice is God's. He has carried it this far and hasn't brought us here to let us fail. The fact that One Voice is where it is points all the more to the love and grace of God.

There is one more area of weakness I want to write about. In the beginning of my ministry, when I started in Elk Grove, I was driven by my passion to see God move. This drive often caused me not to honor the pastors and leaders who were in my life at the time. I know for a fact that I am not the only one who has gone through this. But looking back now, years later, I wish I had "sowed" the honor and respect that was due them, even if I didn't understand.

God places leaders over our lives because, as we grow, those men and women can help us get where we need to be, even though it might not always be the way we want to get there.

I remember when I moved to Los Angeles and started to attend the church that is my home church to this day. When I met the man who would be my pastor I was honest with him, sharing my views of authority and leadership.

"I don't trust you yet," I said to Pastor Netz.

He smiled at me as though he knew something I didn't know.

"It will take time," I added.

He smiled again and then he said, "Let me show you that you can trust me."

What neither of us knew at the time was that his response would lead us into years of discipleship. He was extending his offer of fathering; it was up to me to accept that offer and stop being a lone ranger.

The Bible says in the book of Joel that old men will dream dreams and young men will see visions. This is crucial for us to understand. Old men's dreams become young men's visions. But if young men refuse to come under fathering, many dreams will not be passed down.

I am thankful now more than ever for the men who discipled me, even though at the time I could not understand what God was forming in my life. I realize that I am teaching my team the things I was taught by my first two youth pastors after being saved.

If we can learn to honor the past moves of God and learn to trust Jesus in the leadership He places over us for the future—the men and women who will demonstrate Christ—then I truly believe men and women will come forth who will not only initiate moves of God but sustain them.

And that's where the fruit grows.

Don't run from opportunities to share your weakness. It may be the very thing that brings hope to the hearts of many. And as God continues to save thousands of students across the country, we want them to know the areas of weakness God has brought us from.

Because more than anything else, these point them to Christ.

15

NIGHT
OF HOPE

WHAT MORE COULD WE POSSIBLY dream for high school campuses? Our One Voice team had seen some of the biggest Jesus Clubs in the nation come into being. Not only was our team seeing high school gyms and auditoriums filled with praying students, but the leaders we trained to go into schools throughout Los Angeles were witnessing the same thing.

For three years, from 2013 to 2016, we ministered faithfully to the Roosevelt High campus. Week after week, message after message, we watched as student after student was saved. Yet we knew there was something new that God wanted to do.

Through a divine move of the Lord, I met a man I had looked up to for years. The living faith and personal example of Nick Vujicic have impacted millions all over the world.

I wondered how I would ever meet him.

Well, in July 2015, I found myself in a room sharing my story with Nick. Through a "God moment," we both realized that we were being called to run together to reach campuses.

About this time, our One Voice team began to dream of holding a Youth Crusade after school in Roosevelt High. For a few years now the Lord had been showing us that students are the *heart* of every city and their families are the *body*. If you get the heart you naturally get the body.

So we began to wonder what would happen if students from all over Los Angeles brought their families to events at the schools? What if Jesus Clubs were only the beginning of massive gatherings that would spill over and fill auditoriums or even football fields?

We decided to find out.

Through much prayer and discussion we chose April 1, 2016, as the day for our first Youth Crusade. We would call it "Night of Hope."

It just so happened that this date fell two weeks before Azusa Now, a massive gathering led by Lou Engle that would be taking place in the Memorial Coliseum in L.A.

When we asked Nick Vujicic if he would come and preach the Gospel, he said yes. We were honored that this man who has preached to six hundred million people would come to East L.A.

We then got permission to hold the crusade in the auditorium at Roosevelt, which would hold sixteen hundred people, for that Friday night. We spent the next few months promoting the event—letting students and the community know there was going to be a time and place where they could come and hear a message of hope, which we knew was the Good News of Jesus. We contacted a number of ministries as well, asking them to bring unsaved youth.

By the end of March, fifteen hundred had pre-registered. People were actually planning to come! We didn't know how many were going to show up total; I have found, living in L.A., that it's impossible to judge actual attendance by registration. All we knew was that Jesus wanted the simple message of hope to be proclaimed not just to students in East Los Angeles but also to their families.

What a "God strategy"!

And in all places!

Very often I was brought back to the "323" dream I had had six years earlier and wondered if this was part of what God had been speaking for Roosevelt High.

On the morning of April 1, we all headed to the school for setup. I was completely overwhelmed by the unity I saw as ministries from all over came to help. Many of them were in town for Azusa Now. People from TheCall, Fearless Church from L.A., Youth With A Mission, Circuit Riders and many more were working together as we hoped for a great harvest that night of souls to come to Jesus.

As 6:30 p.m. drew near, I kept going through my routine checkups. As I walked out the front doors of the two-story building that housed the auditorium, I was shocked to see the line wrapped around the quad with students upon students and their families. My heart rejoiced at this sight.

They are coming! I thought. *This is wild. Jesus is becoming famous in East Los Angeles! Tonight heaven is going to throw a party for the souls that are about to come to Christ.*

When I walked onto the stage with my wife, Marcela, and our daughter, Zoe, to introduce the worship team from Fearless Church, I could hardly believe my eyes. Almost every seat was filled and still people were crowding into the auditorium.

I looked out at the faces and saw many students that I passed on campus every week, many who had not come to the Jesus Club. I am not sure if they fully understood what they were there for. Maybe they thought it was a party, as they were clapping and moving with the beat of the techno music we were playing. But, regardless, they were going to encounter the presence of this Man named Jesus.

For the next twenty minutes, Fearless L.A.'s worship team led the people in honoring the name of Jesus. From power songs that caused joy and jumping to slow music that caused our hearts to think about what Jesus had done and the price He had paid for our lives, God's presence was tangible. The stage was being set for the message of hope to be released.

As the music was ending, I stood there on the side of the stage thinking to myself, *Jesus, how did I get here? How did You do this?*

I looked out and saw more than sixteen hundred people who had gathered on a Friday night to hear a message of hope.

And oh, were they going to hear it!

As I was about to introduce Nick, I went to the side of the stage to have a quick word with him. I shared all the excitement I had and how I couldn't believe we had filled the auditorium. He smiled as he always does with me and encouraged my heart to keep going and dreaming for more.

When the worship came to an end, I knew it was my cue to go out and introduce Nick.

It felt as though the atmosphere had changed.

I really believe there are moments when all of heaven leans over to witness salvation through Jesus happen on the earth. I also believe that in these moments all of hell trembles as its grip begins to loosen on those lives it had held captive for years.

"Can you give it up for Nick Vujicic?" I shouted to the crowd. Within seconds, cheers rose up in the room.

As Nick spoke, sharing story after story and pointing every ending to Jesus, you could tell hearts were softening. It was clear that something historic was about to take place. You could literally hear Nick's voice echoing throughout the auditorium.

What a beautiful sound, I thought.

As I looked out over the crowd, my eye caught the founders of the Bible club at Roosevelt, the cousins Sam Alba and Sam Gamboa. They had started the club in the 1970s with faith that it would save many. And once again, on a night of hope, God was continuing to honor their labors.

As Nick was drawing his message to a close, the keyboardist jumped onto the stage and started to play.

Nick began to call for people to give their lives to Jesus. He told them all to join hands; the sounds of many hands joining could be heard throughout the room.

Then he said, "Now, if you have never received Jesus before in your life, I want you to squeeze the hand of the person next to you if you want to receive Him tonight."

Of course, no matter how hard I was trying to see who was squeezing hands, I couldn't.

Then Nick continued, "Now, if someone squeezed your hand, I want you to bring that person up."

It never fails. No matter how many times I see people come to Christ I am amazed. To me it is the greatest miracle on the earth. For a man or woman or boy or girl to surrender his or her life to the Creator is truly astonishing. It's amazing to witness people surrendering their lives to God and trusting Him wholeheartedly.

Many feet began to move as families and students came to the front of the auditorium.

I sat there crying, still in shock as those people gave their lives to Christ that night. All the labor, all the prayers, all the times preaching in this school—it was all worth it. We were now seeing the salvation of students lead to the salvation of families.

What if this were the next new wave of youth ministry in America?

What if waiting for students to come to youth group was no longer appropriate?

What if church plants started to look like youth churches in high schools—gatherings that led to youth crusades filling football stadiums all over America?

That night, sixteen hundred people joined the thousands who have already come forward in a gym or theater or auditorium to meet Jesus since the first Jesus Club meeting in 2009.

Our small One Voice team in Southern California still didn't have all the answers of how our dreams would come true, but we knew we were on the path to what God's heart wanted.

16

MESSAGE TO THE CHURCH

AS THOUSANDS OF STUDENTS AT-tend Jesus Club meetings every week in high schools across California, and now across the country, my heart stirs with faith knowing one thing: God told me the high schools of America would be saved, and that's exactly what He is doing. As of 2016, we are averaging around 10,000 students a week attending Jesus Clubs.

You know, there are two types of words that God gives. The first is the word He gives to an individual that can shape and transform and even change the direction of that person's life.

The second type of word He gives to an individual is not just for that person's life but for his whole generation. It's kind of like the football player who gets the next play from the coach on the sidelines and has to run to his team and relay it to them.

In 2009, after God spoke to me about the high schools of America being saved, I was sure of three things.

Number One, I wasn't God's first choice, but I was the one who said yes.

One time after I had preached, I had this young guy come up to me sharing how God had told him to go to the campuses in Elk Grove and that He would save them. The guy's response to God that night was no. He told God it couldn't be done.

As I stood there hearing him state this, I saw tears of regret begin to fill his eyes.

"Congratulations," he said. "You're doing what I was called to do."

I may not have been God's first choice, but I did say yes and made myself available.

Number Two, the schools were going to be saved.

And Number Three, there was no way this was going to happen by my preaching in every high school in America.

The Lord already had a plan in place to get it done. It is called the Church.

And for such a powerful plan, He had to take His Bride and empower her to bear witness to the beauty of her Groom. Who better to tell this generation about Jesus than those who have met Him?

I'm not talking about a certain structure or building. I'm not talking about a certain ministry style. I'm not talking about Baptist, charismatic, Pentecostal, evangelical or any other stream you can mention.

I'm talking about the Body of Christ worldwide. Those who call Jesus their Savior.

One Voice realizes that the Church as a whole is desperately needed to speak the truth into the lives of young people today. With millions of students in America—15 million, to be exact—there is not one organization that can fit them all into its building.

What if God has positioned the Church of America so that her mission field doesn't require a plane ticket, but just a drive down the street? When I met with Daniel Kolenda in the summer of 2015—Daniel is president of Christ for All Nations (CFAN), a ministry that has led more than 75 million people to the Lord in Africa—he told me that today is a new day for youth ministry in America, referring to what God is doing on high school campuses. When he said that, I thought I knew exactly what he was talking about. For the past several years, we have seen one thing consistently. Students will gather every week to hear the Gospel *when the Gospel is brought to them*. The lie that they don't want Jesus is being washed away by the testimonies taking place all over the nation, as thousands are giving their lives to Him.

This is the change we are seeing in the model of youth ministry in America as churches go to high schools every week, seeing them as their mission fields. Our goal as the Church might no longer be to get students into our buildings, but rather to go where they are, to plant youth churches in every high school in America under the covering and blessing of local churches.

It is no longer our One Voice team alone doing this. In Los Angeles we see this happening all over as people we train go to schools every week and see God save hundreds.

Jesus said the world will know us by our love. But how will the world know our love when we keep it hidden and restricted to a Sunday morning service or Wednesday night youth group?

To every pastor and youth pastor, missionary, church leader or believer reading this, I want to encourage you that a whole nation of students needs you. High schools are waiting for you; they just don't know it yet. Gyms and theaters and auditoriums are waiting for your voice to relay the truth and bring the message of salvation.

Jesus said there will come a time when it is night and no one can work. I believe that America is in darkness, but it's not night yet. I can't tell you how much longer we will have religious freedom to keep preaching the Gospel in high schools, but why wait until it is no longer permitted and we all stand there with regret for what we could have done?

God's divine plan to reach His children is *you*.

Don't believe that students don't want Jesus; they have probably just never met anyone who looks like Him. So go and be that representative at the high school down the street. You never know who might be sitting in your meeting, and who might hear the truth, and what impact that one will have for Jesus.

Years of prayer, intercession and prophecies for California are now being fulfilled. I know that what we are seeing has nothing to do with our strategy or method. It's only that we said yes to God. And God is honoring the promises He made to the saints before our time to save these students: The foundation under our evangelism is decades of prayer for America.

Many have said that another great awakening is coming to America. I want to be bold and say that I believe it's here. The awakening in thousands of kids' hearts is taking place as the message of Jesus is preached and they—along with their families—are getting saved.

We are in what I feel is a window of opportunity. We are in a window of grace and mercy to reach our schools. It's as if a church-planting movement is happening. And we are able in our generation to witness this great work of God.

In 1963 Martin Luther King gave a speech, and a nation broke free from its public segregation. Meanwhile, that same year, another voice broke covenant with God, removing His Word from our schools. These two voices happened to arise at the same point in history, showing me something: God always has a counter for what the enemy is doing.

We live in a day marked by school shootings, as if they are perversely "normal." Drug use is at its highest. Gangs are consistently making more disciples than the Church.

But, once again, the voices are about to clash. A sound will come from the youth of America that will shake the world. This sound to follow Jesus will be stronger than the sound of culture, more powerful than the call of ISIS, and more trustworthy than any lie being fed to our youth today.

On one side, an antichrist spirit speaks to this culture and generation, proclaiming that there are many ways to live and that God approves of sin (even though the

Bible clearly says this is not true). Voices in the world have lied to kids, saying they are gods and can look no further than themselves to find truth.

But on the other side, people are answering the call of our time to reach those students at any cost. On the altar of sacrifice we lay our time and money, knowing that the Word of God will not come back void.

And fifty years from now, a new generation will read of the courageous Church that took a stand and brought forth the Gospel message of Jesus—a time that, I believe, history will know as the Second Jesus Movement.

High schools are a mission field that the Church of America is being called to. It is true that this mission field exists because the Church failed to be present in the years prior. But with no shame or condemnation, we can work together boldly, congregation with congregation, standing on the truth that Jesus Christ is worthy of the worship of every student in this nation.

Then, from the high schools, we will see students answer the call to the nations and reach the unreached people groups. What was once an intimidating giant will be brought down by a stone called *belief*, thrown from the hand of a young generation.

These students need to be given identity and purpose. High schools are a special mission field, because the harvest becomes the laborers for the next harvest. The ones who sit in Jesus Clubs today will be the ones leading the next generations of students.

We at One Voice hear God telling us that high schools will be one of the top-fueling groups of missionaries going out to the unreached internationally—while also reaching our own cities and towns and neighborhoods.

The first student volunteer movement came when college kids gave their lives fearlessly to take the Good News to other countries. I believe the next wave of the best and brightest will come from our high schools.

For many of you reading this book, I believe this to be your call.

You must let your heart awaken to loving this generation. As Loren Cunningham, founder of YWAM, would say: To love God is to make Him known. Remember this simple truth.

This is not the end of this story. This is the beginning of your response to the call of God to the high schools in your neighborhood. I look forward to hearing all that God will do.

This book is about a move of God emerging in California as the Holy Spirit leads. It does not end with one author. There will be many authors of this movement.

The virtual pen is now being passed to anyone who dares to go into a high school and share the love of Christ.

If you are willing to obey, God will take you the rest of the way.

Brian Barcelona is the visionary founder of One Voice Student Missions. He was an atheist who in 2007, at age sixteen, had an encounter with God that changed his life forever. Brian first received his call from God to reach high schools in 2009 and has given his life since then to reach students all over America. Brian's passion is that every high school student in the nation—and the nations—will hear the Good News of Jesus and be saved, discipled and sent out.

One Voice Student Missions was founded in Northern California with Brian and a group of high school students. He started by preaching the Gospel in the high schools there and began seeing thousands saved. Jesus Clubs grew as big as six hundred students gathering every week during lunch on various high school campuses.

Brian and his wife, Marcela, along with their daughter live in Los Angeles, California, with their missional community, One Voice Student Missions.

Connect with Brian and One Voice:
Website: onevoicestudentmissions.com
Facebook: Brianovp and 1OneVoice
Instagram: brianbarcelona and
onevoicestudentmissions
Twitter: @barcelonabrian and @OneVoiceStudent

CPSIA information can be obtained
at www.ICGtesting.com
Printed in the USA
LVHW01s2353261017
553969LV00001B/94/P